PIVOTAL
MOMENTS

Minneapolis, Minnesota

FIRST EDITION EDITION 2025
Pivotal Moments. The Springboard to New Possibilities.
Copyright © 2025 by Jill Konrath, All rights reserved.

No part of this publication may be reproduced, stored in a retrieval system, or transmitted, in any form or by any means, electronic, mechanical, photocopying, recording, or otherwise, without the prior written permission of the author.

ISBN: 978-1-962834-62-9
10 9 8 7 6 5 4 3 2 1

Book cover by Josh Weber
Book design by Gary Lindberg

Praise for *Pivotal Moments*

"Every day is a decision. But nowhere is the impact of those decisions more profound or more variable than in the sometimes obvious, but often subtle moments Jill Konrath calls 'pivotal moments.' Those moments can set you on a path to fulfillment and happiness, but only if you know how to recognize and respond with clear purpose. With Jill Konrath as your guide, this book is your next, best Pivotal Moment."

- BRENT ADAMSON, author of *The Challenger Sale* and *The Framemaking Sale*

"Ever had a gut-punch moment in your career? It could be your biggest opportunity—you just can't see it yet. If you've got goals, ambition, and a hunger to grow, this is your playbook. It's packed with hard-earned wisdom, fresh perspectives, and useful tools to turn 'what happened to me' into 'what made me.'"

- LAUREN BAILEY (LB), Founder, Factor 8, #GirlsClub & Legacy Executive Club

"In this practical and inspiring book about pivotal moments, Jill Konrath shares fresh perspectives, real-life examples, and helpful exercises to help you create positive change—in your own life and in our evolving world."

- MARK ROBERGE, Co-founder at Stage 2 Capital, Professor at HBS, Founding CRO at HubSpot

"*Pivotal Moments* is more than a book—it's a mirror, a map, and a movement. Aligned with Konrath's mission to "inspire positive change in an evolving world," this powerful read invites us to reframe life's turning points as springboards to transformation. As someone who deeply believes in the power of pivotal moments, this book is a profound reminder that our choices shape who we become and how we show up in the world. Whether you're navigating a career shift, personal loss, or yearning for more, you'll find *Pivotal Moments* offers clarity, hope, and a roadmap to your future self."

- HEIDI SOLOMON-ORLICK, Founder of GirlzWhoSell, Author of *Heels to Deals*, *I Have a Voice* and *Just a Dot? I Think Not!*

"Life is full of possibilities. Putting yourself in a position for as many pivotal moments as you can will take you to places where you'll thrive. This book will make your head spin with ideas."
- FRED DIAMOND, Founder, Institute for
Effective Professional Selling

"In *Pivotal Moments*, motivational author and speaker Jill Konrath moves beyond the arena of sales to explore the deeper realm of the human experience in moments of change. Her mix of memoir and philosophy shows that the magic of pivotal moments is not in having them but recognizing and acting on them. Stories come through a rear-view mirror—the book features more than 30 such inspirational moments of how a wide variety of people survived and grew from personal challenges."
- LINDA RICHARDSON, Founder Richardson, consultant, and author
of NYT best-selling *Changing the Sales Conversation*
and many other sales books.

"Jill Konrath has turned her own life's pivotal moments into the kind of inspiring and practical book you will want to dip into again and again, each time finding new tidbits to savor. Brava!"
- HILDY GOTTLIEB, Co-Founder of CreatingtheFuture.org,
TEDx speaker, author, and developer of Catalytic Thinking

"I've known Jill Konrath for more than a decade, not just as a bestselling author, but as a friend whose wisdom has guided me through my own pivotal moments. *Pivotal Moments* is Jill at her most grounded and generous. She shows us how to recognize when we've hit the wall, how to listen when life whispers "something has to change," and how to move forward with both courage and clarity. The 75% Excitement / 25% Fear rule is a powerful compass for choosing what comes next."
- SHARI LEVITIN, LinkedIn Top Voice, Speaker,
author of *Heart and Sell*

PIVOTAL MOMENTS

The Springboard to New Possibilities

JILL KONRATH

Minneapolis, Minnesota

Also by Jill Konrath

Selling to Big Companies (2005)

SNAP Selling: Speed Up Sales and Win More Business with Today's Frazzled Customers (2012)

Agile Selling: Get Up to Speed Quickly in Today's Ever-Changing Sales World (2014)

More Sales, Less Time: Surprisingly Simple Strategies for Today's Crazy-Busy Sellers (2016)

Pivotal Moments is dedicated to you—because your life matters and so much more is possible.

The frog is the emblem of transformation. It symbolizes major life changes, personal growth and renewal.

Table of Contents

Introduction 1

PART 1 – GETTING STARTED 5

Chapter 1 – What Do You Really Want? 7
Chapter 2 – Hitting the Wall 11
Chapter 3 – Surviving the Jolt 15
Chapter 4 – Lighting the Spark 19
Chapter 5 – Creating an Adventure 25

PART 2 – BOUNCING FORWARD 31

Chapter 6 – Reflecting on Life 33
Chapter 7 – Looking Inside 39
Chapter 8 – Gaining Clarity 46
Chapter 9 – Tapping Into Community 50
Chapter 10 – Envisioning Possibilities 55

PART 3 – CREATING YOUR FUTURE 59

Chapter 11 – Designing Your Plan 61
Chapter 12 – Reducing Gulp Moments 67
Chapter 13 – Getting More "AHAs" 73
Chapter 14 – Dancing With Discouragement 79
Chapter 15 – Enjoying Serendipity 82
Chapter 16 – Blazing a New Trail 89

PART 4 – INSPIRING ACTION 91

Pivotal Moment Stories 93

Chapter 17 – Finding Unstoppable Ideas 95

When No Became My Starting Point – Angela Botiba 96

Shifting Gears – Risa August 99

My Mess Became My Ministry – Melinda Emerson 102

Tithing My Time – Todd Johnson 105

The Silver Lining to Getting Sacked – Joanne Black 108

Finding My "No-Fear" Footing – Ardath Albee 111

Chapter 18 – Gaining New Perspectives 115

Dao's Defining Moment – Dao Jensen 116

The Question that Lit a Spark – Orrin Broberg 118

I Was Determined – Lori Chester 121

Rule One Magic – Dawn Epstein 125

Up the Hill – Colleen Stanley 127

Breaking Out of Poverty Required Heartbreaking Decisions – Michael Nelson 130

Chapter 19 – Embracing Opportunities 133

Pivoting Into the Startup World – Dan Tyre 134

My Worst Christmas Gift Became My Greatest Fortune – Joe Yun 137

The First Step Forward – Lori Harris 140

When a War Changes Your Map – Yuliia Yurchuk 143

The Award That Changed Everything – Luke Goetting 146

It Started on a Ski Lift – Dave Brock 149

Chapter 20 – Getting Unstuck 153

    The Ultimate Pivot – Tom Morris 154

    The Moment I Stopped Pretending – Colleen Kranz 156

    I Thought I Wasn't Capable Until... – Robert Middleton 158

    Letting Go of My Father – Jonathan London 161

    Life's Not Punishing You, It's Growing You – Stephen Moegling 164

Chapter 21 – Finding Fullness 169

    The Hole in My Heart – Shari Levitin 170

    The Gift of Rejection – Keith Becker 173

    Thank God I Didn't Get the Scholarship – Josh LaBau 176

    The Day I Left for Good – Lori Richardson 178

    Love Makes a Family: The Story of JJ – Carlos Quintero 180

    He Left Me for Eight Months – Janellen Brock 182

PART 5 – SPRINGING FORWARD 185

Chapter 22 – Taking Action 187

Acknowledgements 189

About the Author 190

Introduction

It was the middle of the night. I was sound asleep when suddenly I woke up. An idea for a new book was practically bursting in my head. I got up, went to the living room, and began jotting down my thoughts.

For days on end, I was immersed in this new endeavor. Though I'd never written fiction before, I was thoroughly enjoying envisioning the scenario, plotline, and characters. I took pages and pages of notes as I scoped out how the story would unfold.

But just a few weeks later, all that changed. I was awakened from a deep sleep by a voice that spoke to me in a very authoritative manner. "NO! I COME FIRST!" it said. I was in shock; this was not a normal occurrence. Then the voice spoke again. "PIVOTAL MOMENTS," it declared, as if it were a foregone conclusion.

With a personal mission to "Inspire positive change in an evolving world," I intuitively felt that a higher power was directing me to write a book on pivotal moments instead. Although that thought had never crossed my mind, I knew it was something I had to do, having experienced so many pivotal moments in my life.

But what exactly is a pivotal moment? It's when something happens that triggers a change in your life. It could be an insight or a realization. It could be related to your career. Maybe something happens to your family or health. Whatever it is, going backwards isn't an option.

Starting a new endeavor or changing directions in your life can feel overwhelming. Your emotions might be all over the place. You could be uncertain about which path to take. Considering all the consequences takes time. Additionally, deep introspection is necessary to align with what's important to you and ensure you're prepared for it.

Pivotal moments always elicit angst, too. You could question your abilities. You worry about the impact on others. You could be fretting over your finances. Plus, making changes while managing a busy life is tough, especially when your current job or obligations drain your energy.

I know. I've been there and done that many times over the years. Believe it or not, I've learned a lot about what it takes to succeed when you're taking these kinds of risks.

The truth is, starting is often the most challenging part. To get this book started, I escaped briefly to a family cabin in northern Minnesota during a bitterly cold winter. That pretty much guaranteed that no one would drop in to interrupt my thinking.

That's when I decided that Pivotal Moments needed to be filled with fresh strategies and practical advice you could use right away. As you read it, you'll discover how to:

- Restart yourself after hitting the wall.
- Find the hidden opportunities you might not see.
- Develop more viable options for moving forward.
- Navigate the challenges you encounter.
- Create a happier, more satisfying life.

I want to fill you with inspiration too! I've shared many personal stories about my challenging moments, the decisions I made, and how I created an upward spiral in my life. Plus, I've included 29 stories from friends, colleagues, and strangers to give you more ideas about how you can create the life you want.

Finally, be sure to check out the resources in Part 5. They'll help you gain a deeper insight into yourself, the choices in front of you, and what it'll take to make your future even brighter.

May this book uplift and inspire you as you strive to create what's really possible in your life.

It's time to make that big leap forward!

Part 1
Getting Started

Chapter 1
What Do You Really Want?

Big question—and surprisingly tough to answer. Each of us aspires and dreams about how we want our lives to unfold. Over time, these evolve. But it's challenging to understand what's genuinely possible in your life until you've gained some experience.

In sixth grade, my teacher asked our class to write about what we wanted to be when we grew up. I struggled with the assignment. I couldn't decide if I wanted to be the first woman on Mars, an interpreter at the United Nations, or a senator from the great state of Minnesota.

Clearly, I'm a miserable failure—at least so far. And while all are still hypothetically achievable, they no longer have any appeal.

But imagine saying this in the future: "I've had an incredible life. Even those downtimes I had, the insecurities I dealt with, and the detours I went through were worth it. I learned so much from them. I wouldn't be who I am today without having those experiences."

That's what we're aiming for in Pivotal Moments. While life is a challenge, viewing it from a different perspective can also make it immensely fun and rewarding.

So, how do you create this desired future? It starts with recognizing that we live in a time of uncertainty. Our world is swirling. This past year, many people were laid off. Yet, despite the tough job market, Inc. magazine reported that sixty percent of employees want a new job. Why? Work-life balance, job security, more interesting work, career growth opportunities, higher salaries, and improved benefits.

In short, they're looking for something better. If you're not feeling satisfied with the direction your life is taking, it's crucial to define what would make you happy. Fortunately, Arthur Brooks, Harvard Business School professor and author of *The Happiness Files*, has done extensive research on this topic.

According to Brooks, by using his '75% Excitement, 25% Fear Rule" when considering a change in your life, you can make better decisions about which direction to take. As you evaluate each option, think about these factors.

- 75% Excitement: The direction you're thinking about energizes you, makes you feel motivated, and eager to get started down this new path.
- 25% Fear: The direction you're considering taking gets you out of your comfort zone—yet you see a real opportunity for personal growth or mastery of a new skill.
- 0% Deadness: If you're feeling apathetic or have a sense of deadness, you definitely won't be happy with your life.

Imagine applying that "75/25 Rule" to your life today. What would you do differently? What changes would you make? What would you eliminate? How could you set yourself up to ensure that excitement occurs more often?

If you overlook these factors, you risk facing a pivotal moment that might lead you to reassess many aspects of your life. Things may be tough, but they also have the potential to improve your future.

Some pivotal moments are truly significant and cannot be ignored. They may hit you over the head, forcing you to change what you're doing. Other pivotal moments are whispers that nudge you to do something different.

What causes them? If you're like most people, you begin down one path because it seems right at the time—and it pays the bills. Or perhaps you had no idea what you wanted, so you took what was available. However, you may also have lacked the resources and support to pursue something different.

You may wake up one day and decide you can't tolerate what you're doing anymore. Or you'll see that your relationships could be so much better. You might be kicked out of your comfort zone and forced to take a new direction. You may suddenly have an idea or an epiphany that sends you down a different path. Even better, someone says something to you that alters your perception of who you are and your capabilities.

In short, these pivotal moments are turning points that lead to a noticeable and lasting change in your life or situation. A new phase is starting. It's both exciting and scary.

With a pivotal moment, you're also faced with new decisions that impact you and others. You'll have moments of clarity at the same time you worry about your ability to carry it off. As you work towards turning your new focus into reality, you'll go through numerous ups and downs.

Walking into the unknown is like that. But if you've embraced a pivotal moment, you'll have a gut feeling that you're headed in the right direction. You'll have lots to learn along this journey, but at your core, you'll know it's right. Even if it requires work, involves risk, or is super challenging.

Choosing to embrace these pivotal moments also impacts your personal life. They make you a better, stronger person, more in tune with what you love, what types of contributions you want to make, and even the kind of people you choose to hang out with.

Unleashing an upward spiral in your life requires a new way of thinking. It's all about focusing on "what's really possible" rather than limiting yourself to what you already know.

It's about turning challenging situations into occasions for growth. It's about identifying and capitalizing on hidden opportunities.

Take a moment now to consider which part of your life you might want to change or could be fun to change. Once you make that decision, you can begin this new journey. It may take some time to build your new reality, and there will be stepping stones along the way.

That's just the way it is. But at least you'll be headed in the right direction. Up, up, up!

In the upcoming chapters, we'll take a deeper look at the impetus behind the most common pivotal moments, share real-life stories, and introduce strategies you can use to take advantage of the moment.

Chapter 2
Hitting the Wall

It happens to all of us. We stay too long in what we're doing. We know it deep down. We're not happy with our work, our relationships, or our careers. We stay because we've already invested a lot of time, effort, and emotional energy in trying to make things work.

We're paralyzed. We don't want to rock the boat. We're afraid of the unknown and the judgment or rejection of others. Additionally, we may face potential financial instability.

In our minds, the possibility of failure looms large. Facing this "status quo" bias is a real challenge, especially when we lack a clear idea of what to do next. Figuring that out takes a lot of energy and effort. So, we rationalize staying put while disregarding any future costs and benefits.

In short, we do nothing—until one day, something snaps inside us. We've hit the proverbial wall. But now, where do we even start?

Time for a Change

I remember the first time it happened to me. After a few years of teaching and coaching at a high school, I was miserable. It clearly was the wrong job for me. I felt constrained, as I was unable to make any changes to the designated curriculum to increase learning and student engagement. I was going nuts.

So, I started looking for a new job. After a few months, it became clear to me that no one was interested in hiring me. Even my "in" with the VP of a regional bank turned into nothing. He thought I'd make an excellent teller because I had a great smile. So, I went back to my teaching job and was even more miserable.

After my second summer of job hunting, I decided to start my own company. At the time, I didn't know anyone who had done that, but I was determined to make it happen.

I spent months at the local library reading business magazines and taking notes on anything that caught my interest. I hoped to discover something that would inspire an idea for starting a company.

Then, one day, the lightbulb went on. Two statistics I'd uncovered crashed together:

1. Companies were having trouble relocating executives for the first time. These men now had working wives, so uprooting the entire family was a significant issue.
2. The Minneapolis/St. Paul area, where I lived, had the sixth-largest concentration of corporate headquarters in the United States.

Putting two and two together, I realized that I could work with these big companies, helping spouses find employment and ensuring that all family needs (e.g., horseback riding lessons, daycare, and art teachers) were met.

I roped in two friends to help me pursue this concept. Then, I studied how to write a business plan—something I had no prior knowledge about—and put one together.

Finally, I set up a meeting with SCORE, a government agency that helps small businesses get started. We met with a retired Vice President of Marketing from General Mills.

After presenting our plan to him, he said it was a timely, much-needed idea. And, probably most importantly, he thought we could do it! I was elated.

Then, he looked at us and said, "Now, which one of you three will be doing the sales?"

I looked at him in shock. Sales? Nothing could be more disgusting to me than being in sales. They were all a bunch of pushy peddlers.

I leaned forward in horror and said, "I thought you said it was a good idea?"

He replied, "It is Jill. But someone has to sell it."

I told him we'd have to discuss that among ourselves. Later, when I had that conversation with my future partners, it was clear that they detested sales even more than I did.

After reflecting on it for a while, I ultimately concluded that it had to be me. It was my idea. I was the driving force. I needed to find a sales job. It didn't happen overnight. I explored a few paths that didn't feel right. But I kept at it.

Ultimately, my perseverance was rewarded. I was hired by Xerox, a company that at the time had one of the best sales training programs in the world. I discovered that good salespeople aren't sleazy. They're focused on helping customers achieve their goals and objectives.

I fell in love with sales and never returned to my initial idea. But all that effort was worth it because it opened a career path for me that I could never have imagined.

In the years that followed, I established a consulting business, authored five business books, and presented at international conferences worldwide. As I said, it was time to change. I couldn't have known what was in store for me back then, but I knew I needed to act.

***

Hitting the wall isn't easy, but it's clearly a pivotal moment that drives people to explore options they've never considered before.

It may be the type of work you're doing that brings you no satisfaction. Maybe it's just the wrong job for you. Or you realize that it's a total dead-end. You could be in a toxic work environment or relationship that crushes your spirit, saps your energy, and negatively impacts your health.

Whatever the reason, it's time to make the move. And the best thing is, when one door closes, a new one opens. In the following chapters, I promise you'll find plenty of ideas on how to unleash your best potential.

Chapter 3
Surviving the Jolt

There's nothing worse than getting kicked out of your comfort zone when you think things are going pretty well in your life. It's like a sucker punch to your belly. You weren't expecting it, and it hurts like crazy.

These jolts can come in many forms. Perhaps your company is downsizing. One day, you get called into the office—or check your email—to find out that you are no longer employed. You might have suspected it was coming but still hoped you wouldn't be cut. Suddenly, you're faced with new problems that you're not prepared for.

Health challenges can affect you in the same way. Not only do they take you out for a while, but they may even threaten your very livelihood. You might be faced with family issues such as divorce, death, or a slew of other things. Weather problems, such as wildfires, hurricanes, or tornadoes, can change everyone's priorities overnight.

When the jolt hits, all you can think about is, "Now what?" There's no going back. There's only going forward, and for a while, you spin in place. Confused, unsure, scared.

The answers don't come quickly. It's hard to shift yourself into a problem-solving mode. Sometimes, you need to spend time grieving what's gone and what will never be.

I've been there a few times in my life and, fortunately, survived. However, it's not easy because it requires some deep thinking about who you are, what you want to do, the resources available to you, and the people around you.

Professionally, I faced a massive career crisis a while back. At that time, I was working with my two largest clients and was booked solid for the next six months. Suddenly, everything came to a screeching halt. The country went into a recession. Under pressure from Wall Street to deliver better earnings, both companies had to cut all extraneous expenses.

My consulting projects evaporated overnight. My clients said, "Hang in there, Jill. We'll restart soon." They never did.

Suddenly, I was thrust back into prospecting mode again. I quickly discovered that the approach I'd used with great success for many years was grossly ineffective. At first, I was frustrated, but as time passed, my fears began to run rampant.

I worried that I'd lost my mojo and no one would ever hire me again. After all, who wants to work with a sales consultant who can't get clients?

Even when well-intentioned friends offered ideas, I was pessimistic and dismissive. I was caught in a downward spiral of negativity. Just when I needed all the brainpower I could muster, it was unavailable to me.

Finally, I began asking other entrepreneurs and salespeople if they were experiencing any issues. It was like opening a floodgate. Everyone I spoke to was struggling; recessions do that to people.

For the first time, I realized that it wasn't all about me. That was a real relief! Other factors were at play. The game had changed, and I needed to learn the new rules.

Just as I was mentally recovering, I got hit with another jolt. While coming home from a class reunion—and having a bit too much to drink—I got a DWI and lost my license. I was totally humiliated. I didn't want to face the world. I didn't want anyone to know, except my teenage kids. They needed to hear about it because if it happened to me, it could easily happen to them.

In the following year, I had to get rides to court hearings and to be tested for drugs and alcohol. When I finally secured new clients, it was tough to meet with them as well. All this was before Zoom and Uber, so I had to figure out new ways to do my consulting work. Rather than meeting in person (which was expected of consultants), I switched virtually all of them to phone conversations.

With jolts like the ones I just described, you face a choice. Do you simply accept the situation and lower your expectations? Or do you rethink your priorities, ways of working, relationships, and more?

I chose to take action and ultimately staged a comeback that surpassed anything I could have ever imagined. Was it hard? Yes. Was it challenging? Yes. Did it happen overnight? No. Was it worthwhile? Yes, yes, a hundred times yes.

Then, just as I was at the peak of my career, my late husband died unexpectedly from a complication of his liver disease. At the same time, my mother's Alzheimer's disease kicked into high gear, and my father was in and out of the hospital. Both passed away within the next two years. Once more, it was a significant jolt. Unexpected, but that's life. It took some time to bounce back, but I'm here again.

The truth is, we all face jolts. It's not if, it's when. That's the joy and the challenge of being human. As you can imagine, throughout the years, I've developed various strategies for navigating difficult times in our lives.

Chapter 4
Lighting the Spark

There's nothing more exciting than getting an idea. Often, it begins as just a glimmer that quickly flits into your consciousness and then moves on. You may even miss it the first time. Over time, it may pop back into your mind with a slightly different twist. That idea of yours is trying hard to capture your attention.

So, you start thinking about it more and more. You conduct research. You start bouncing it off others. The more you do that, the more the idea gels in your mind. Ultimately, you need to get started turning it into a reality. Step-by-step.

Other times, the idea comes from a comment someone has made to you. I'll never forget my conversation with Bob, a human resources consultant.

After taking a hiatus following the birth of my second child, I started a training company. With my background, it seemed like a no-brainer career decision. While I had decent clients, I wasn't thrilled with the work. Something was wrong.

That's when I bumped into Bob in the parking lot. He was visiting a mutual friend in our shared office. He greeted me with a big smile and asked, "How's it going?" Before I knew it, I was blurting out all the fears racing through my mind.

"I'm scared to death," I confessed. "I love learning new things, experimenting to see what works best, and sharing it with others. But after that, I'm bored. Bored stiff. It's a curse—a bad one. You can't succeed in any job if you don't stick around to capitalize on what you've learned. I'm headed for a downward spiral."

That's when Bob butted in, "Jill, I work with lots of different companies. They need people who can quickly analyze a situation, search for alternative approaches, and lead others in a new direction. It's your strength."

I was shocked. I wasn't used to seeing my worst quality as my biggest asset. But before long, I refocused my efforts on new product launches—all new, all the time. I was in heaven, doing my best work. Additionally, my clients appreciated it because I could help them quickly achieve their objectives.

As I mentioned earlier, my business crashed. I'd been going gangbusters for a decade, and it was all gone. I spent months figuring out how to set up meetings with potential clients. No one answered the phone or responded to my emails. Ultimately, I discovered an approach that proved effective.

I realized I had to write a book because many others were struggling. I'd never planned to be an author, but it suddenly occurred to me that I needed to be. I researched how to do that, spoke with a few authors, wrote a proposal, and submitted it to a publisher. Before long, I'd signed a contract.

On the first day, as I sat at my desk to write, I remembered a book I'd read earlier, *Your Highest Goal*. It advises that before starting any major project, ask yourself, "What is my highest goal?"

So, I did. A split second later, I smugly replied, "To show salespeople and entrepreneurs how to sell to big companies." After all, it was the title of the book.

Suddenly, a new thought popped into my head: "No, it isn't." I sat there, stunned. Then, from a deeper place in myself, another thought emerged. My highest goal was to "help people feel that it was possible for them to sell their products or services to larger corporations."

Right away, I realized that this was much more motivating. As I wrote, I needed to share my mistakes first, then explain what worked and why. This made all the difference; people could relate to it. I loved thinking about what was possible, not just what already existed.

Before long, I thought maybe someday I'd write a book called What's Possible. I logged onto GoDaddy to check if I could buy the www.whatspossible.com domain name, but it was already taken. GoDaddy suggested that I might like WhatsReallyPossible.com instead, so I bought it. Now, rather than a book, I have a website where I can continue to share my thoughts and ideas on this topic. However, it took almost twenty years to make it a reality. It's now my passion.

Davide Hume, a Scottish philosopher, once said, "Reason is, and ought only to be the slave of the passions."

It's true. Turning an idea into a reality is a wonderful and time-consuming endeavor. Without passion, the hard work won't be accomplished, and what is created from that passion is infinitely better.

Vani Hari, the Food Babe, is another excellent example of someone who was "sparked" into taking action. I stumbled upon her website years ago. Having a strong interest in nutrition, I signed up for the newsletter.

I was particularly interested in Vani's story. In her early twenties, she was overweight, had low energy, and ultimately, experienced a health crisis that sent her to the hospital. It was then that she decided to make health her number one priority.

She says, "I used my newfound inspiration for living a healthy life to drive my energy into investigating what is really in our food, how it is grown, and what chemicals are used in its production."

She spent hours researching, consulting with experts, reading food labels, and analyzing the marketing of food products. She also put what she learned into practice, which made her feel better, gave her more energy, and led to a greater sense of well-being. Passionate about the changes she had made in her life, she started her blog to share what she learned.

Little did she know where it would lead. When she discovered that many food additives are permitted in the US but banned in Europe due to their adverse health impacts, she took action.

Even better, Vani speaks out about these issues in multiple forums. She testified in the US Senate, spoke at the White House, and been featured on every major news network. Most recently, her efforts have resulted in the FDA banning artificial dyes from our food.

The Food Babe Army she has assembled has also compelled major food companies, including Kraft, Chick-fil-A, Chipotle, Subway, General Mills, Panera Bread, Anheuser-Busch, and Starbucks, to improve their food products, making them safer for everyone.

On her website, Vani shares all her knowledge. You can also find her on multiple social media platforms and numerous podcasts. She's written multiple books. I've even given her cookbooks to my adult children so they can prepare healthy meals for their kids. And now she has even launched her healthy food line.

Becoming an activist wasn't her goal when she started her blog. She just wanted to share what she'd learned. And look where it led. She's making a big difference for all of us.

***

Just think about it. If an idea comes to you, it's truly a gift. Turning it into reality takes time. You learn a lot along the way. Your idea morphs into something better.

Having passion and a purpose for what you're doing sustains you during the early stages and helps you keep going.

But where do these ideas come from? Most people don't realize that there are ways to spark more ideas. You can't just wait for them to appear out of nowhere. And that's a topic we'll be talking about shortly.

Chapter 5
Creating a New Adventure

How can you turn your pivotal moment into an upward spiral filled with new possibilities better than ever imagined? After all, you're likely running a bit scared. You may seriously question your ability to recover from the jolt or to turn your ideas into reality.

What if you decide to go on an adventure instead of letting fear or doubt rule your thinking? That's right, you're heading into new territory where you've never been before. You're not even sure where you're headed, but you're on the way. You may encounter some challenges too.

I'll never forget my first big adventure. I was twenty years old, heading to Europe for three months with two friends. Before we left, we'd arranged to buy a rebuilt Volkswagen station wagon from a mechanic in a small German village. It gave us the ability to go anywhere we wanted at any time. Additionally, we could sleep in the back, which helped keep costs down.

When we arrived, we mapped out a circular route to visit all the "must-see" sites. In addition to driving, we hitchhiked in the UK, took ferries to cross the seas and channels, and occasionally rode a bus. We met incredible people from all over the world. I learned to say, "Where is the bathroom?" in many languages. Then, before we went home, we sold our car for almost what we had paid for it.

However, here are just a few of the exciting and scary parts: an international strike against hijacking delayed my flight to Europe for a day. I had no plans (or cell phones) to meet up with my friends and hoped I could find them.

Driving into Paris, I encountered my very first roundabout. It had over five lanes. I couldn't get out. We went around and around. I was a wreck. In Rome, while visiting the Colosseum, we got caught in what was described as "the rainstorm of the century." Streets were flooded, cars floated by, and giant potholes appeared out of nowhere.

While we were in Morocco, there was an attempt to overthrow the king. Gunfire was heard just a few blocks away. The city was on lockdown for a few days. In Munich, we visited the Olympic Village on the same day that eleven Israeli team members were taken hostage and shot. Security was crazy.

It was quite the adventure. I was way outside of my comfort zone, doing things I wouldn't normally do. But I was open to the experiences it gave me. It also gave me confidence in my ability to handle unexpected and challenging situations.

Since then, I've had many adventures in my profession, relationships, and other areas of life. I've done things I never intended to do but learned a lot in the process. These are just a few of the adventures I went on:

- Create a Job Adventure
- Success in Sales Adventure
- Parenting Adventure
- Consulting Adventure

- Publishing Adventure
- Speaker Adventure

Each was an incredible learning experience, often accompanied by numerous challenges. But success in each adventure gave me the confidence to move forward.

A few years ago, I took another big adventure. After my late husband's death, I needed to create a new life. Living in the outer suburbs was isolating. So was working from a home office. I craved human interaction. That's when I decided to sell my house and buy a downtown condo. My kids were hesitant. They wanted me to rent first and try out city living.

But I was vehement. I told them, "This is Jill's Urban Adventure. I'm not sure if I'll like it, but I'll find out. And, if I rented, I wouldn't commit to making it home or initiating new friendships. If it doesn't work out, I'll figure out what to do next. After all, that's part of the adventure."

Think about it this way: Pivotal moments are the start of your next life adventure. You'll be walking into the future, with wide-eyed wonder, scared about what's ahead. However, this time in your life is truly an opportunity to step up and create your future.

Adventures are filled with learning, trying, testing, and experimenting. They're about looking at the world differently; they serve as springboards to what's next.

Sure, there will be ups and downs, and you'll experience all sorts of emotions. Planning can reduce the risk, but it won't eliminate it. As you learn more about what works best for you, you'll refine your adventure or take it to the next level, spiraling upward.

Don't forget to name your adventure, too! It reminds you that you're on a journey to create fresh possibilities in your life.

So, what adventure are you taking now?

Finally, I want to share the poem below with you. I first heard it in my teens, and over the decades, I've used it many times to bolster my confidence when trying something new.

It Couldn't Be Done
Edgar Guest

Somebody said that it couldn't be done
But he with a chuckle replied
That "maybe it couldn't," but he would be one
Who wouldn't say so till he'd tried.
So he buckled right in with the trace of a grin
On his face. If he worried he hid it.
He started to sing as he tackled the thing
That couldn't be done, and he did it!

Somebody scoffed: "Oh, you'll never do that;
At least no one ever has done it;"
But he took off his coat and he took off his hat
And the first thing we knew he'd begun it.
With a lift of his chin and a bit of a grin,
Without any doubting or quiddit,
He started to sing as he tackled the thing
That couldn't be done, and he did it.

There are thousands to tell you it cannot be done,
There are thousands to prophesy failure,
There are thousands to point out to you one by one,
The dangers that wait to assail you.

But just buckle in with a bit of a grin,
Just take off your coat and go to it;
Just start to sing as you tackle the thing
That "cannot be done," and you'll do it.

PART 2
Bouncing Forward

Chapter 6
Reflecting on Life

Welcome to your era of reinvention. At first, you may be reeling from what recently happened. Or you may be excited about what's coming next. But if you're like most people, you're out of your comfort zone.

Either way, it's time for some introspection. Why? Because pivotal moments are all about decisions. Will you go this way or that way? Will you take action or not? What will you do next? What are the priorities?

But first, looking at where you've come from is essential. Most people don't often reflect on their lives; they're too busy looking forward. They also don't appreciate their journey or all they've learned along the way.

As I was thinking about this book, I started to write down what's taken me to this point in my life. For example, here are just a few...

If I Hadn't...

If I hadn't seen Pollyanna as a child, I would never have learned how to find the upside of the downtimes.

If I hadn't been a waitress in high school and college, I would never have been comfortable talking to so many different people.

If so many companies hadn't rejected me as I was job hunting, I would never have considered starting my own company.

If I hadn't talked to a SCORE advisor, I would never in a million years have gone into sales.

If I hadn't committed to being in sales for just one year, I would never have discovered a good career path that I'd never considered.

If my father hadn't told me he requested a demotion from a management position back to engineering because he loved that job, I wouldn't have had the courage to walk away from the sales management path.

If I hadn't had two babies, I would have never left the corporate world and started my own consulting firm.

If I hadn't been so upset by how few women sales experts were speakers at conferences, featured in magazines, or visible online, I would never have stuck my neck out to be visible.

If my business hadn't failed, I would never have discovered what strategies worked in a changing business environment. Nor would I ever have believed I had enough expertise to write a book about anything.

If I hadn't discovered that my chances of getting a publisher increased if I were a speaker, I would have avoided it at all costs.

If my first book hadn't been successful, I would never have written the following three sales books, traveled to conferences around the world, or had the opportunity to impact so many people positively.

If we hadn't had a country-wide recession, I would never have written a special book for job seekers, held eighteen months of webinars for them, or met so many incredible people.

If three of the most important people in my life hadn't passed away in a short time, I would have continued doing what I was doing instead of taking time to reflect on my future and consider my next steps.

If the country's politics hadn't become so divisive, I would never have launched my WhatsReallyPossible.com website.

If I hadn't encountered a former colleague at an out-of-town conference, I wouldn't have married a wonderful man who supports my initiatives.

If I hadn't moved to a downtown condo, I would have never met such an inspiring group of people who continually motivate me to contribute positively to this world.

**

All these things were pivotal moments in my life. Each one caused me to rethink where I was going in life, what I was good at, and what I sucked at. They impacted the choices I made and my confidence in moving forward.

I've had many more "If I Hadn't" moments. So many that it surprised me. I could see the many challenging situations I've been through before. But it was one step at a time. I could appreciate what I've learned and the risks I've taken.

Knowing all this about ourselves can transform us from survivors to thrivers. Acknowledging the many strengths you already have and what you've accomplished is a significant first step.

Going Quiet

Having time to think is important, and having time to recover is essential if you've just been through a tough spot. Be kind to yourself.

I've walked a few million miles over the past few decades—or so it seems. Getting outside, away from any devices or potential interruptions, and moving does so many things. It opens your mind to new ideas. All those steps have led to some of my best thinking and most creative ideas.

As I write this, I'm planning to take a thirty-minute walk along the Mississippi River to clear my mind and focus on the next chapter.

But walking isn't the only way to be quiet. Taking time to meditate or pray can have huge benefits, too. These practices help you better cope with difficulties. They enhance feelings of gratitude, lift your mood, and give you a deeper sense of purpose.

I've also had to get away to think. The chaos of raising young children made it tough to have coherent thoughts. Over the years, I've rented a hotel room for a few nights to get a jump-start on my thinking. When a good friend was on vacation, I moved in to care for her two cats. I've also spent hours in the quiet of the library, where no one can reach me or interrupt me.

So, put on your thinking cap now and take some time to do a little reflecting on your life.

Your Challenge

1. Create your own "If I Hadn't" poster. Remember, pivotal moments don't have to be huge. But they do have to:

    - Inspire you to go in a new direction.
    - Add value to your current situation.
    - Stretch your capabilities and skills.
    - Challenge your thinking.

2. Ask yourself these questions. As you review your pivotal moments, think about:

   - What did you learn about yourself from them?
   - How did you make the change?
   - What skills did you need to get better at?
   - What did you need to learn? Deepen?
   - How did you get the support you needed?
   - What can you appreciate about yourself that will help you move forward?

3. Relish in your accomplishments. Yup! You deserve it. You've already come a long way. And, by savoring your past successes, you'll be more ready for what lies ahead.

Chapter 7
Looking Inside

It's time for some introspection. We began by looking back at previous pivotal moments so you could reflect on what you've learned and accomplished. But many decisions are still ahead and hope alone won't get you there.

To set ourselves up for success, we need to look inside ourselves. We can learn a great deal about where we want to go, how to get there, and what will lead to our most fulfilling next steps.

Here are some questions that are guaranteed to stimulate your thinking:

When Do You Light Up?

This might be the most important question you could ask. It's what makes you feel alive. Start by thinking about your early years. What was fun, exciting, and interesting to you? Then look at how you felt as you grew older. And finally, think about what you love doing today.

As I reflect, I remember the excitement I felt about attending one of the largest universities in the country. I was eager to shed my high school classmates' perceptions of me and discover who I truly was.

I remember the joy of beginning a career in sales. Every day, I met different people from various companies in entirely different roles. I loved figuring out what it took to be successful in diverse scenarios and then sharing it with my colleagues. As I matured, I ended up writing four books on different sales challenges and then speaking worldwide.

I could go on and on, but there's a theme: exploration, learning, and then sharing what I've learned with others. It's what I love to do.

Your Turn: Think about your favorite memories—the ones you relish. Then ask yourself, "What makes me come alive? When do I light up? What commonalities do I see? How can I incorporate these into my future?"

What Motivates You?

That's another critical question to think about. As it relates to your work or career, you may have one answer. However, when you consider your family, significant relationships, or your health, that introduces an entirely new dimension.

The reality is that there are no universally correct choices; everything is relative to your unique situation and what matters to you.

What follows are several compelling examples of people who truly connected with what motivated them and then turned their passions into a reality.

***

Patricio (Pato) Moo is the founder and director of UluumilKaab, a producer of premium artisan honey in the Yucatán. Years ago, as a teenager, he would drive one and a half hours each way to a job at a resort in Cancún, helping to support his family.

But even back then, Pato had a big dream. His vision was: "To help my fellow villagers thrive by creating a business where they can sell their honey, and build recognition throughout the world, and through our brand, promote our Mayan culture and help preserve our ancestral traditions."

It took him many years to achieve that goal, but his motto during that whole time was this: "I don't care. I will do it. I am ready." It was a family endeavor, but Pato's vision kept it alive.

Take time to ask yourself, "What motivates me?" By understanding your "why," you'll remain motivated even in tough times. You'll acquire the necessary knowledge. Step by step, you'll make progress and engage others in your vision. Everyone gains from this.

What Would You Do Even If You Didn't Get Paid?

What you volunteer for reflects your passions and the motivations behind your actions. Consider the organizations you volunteer for, the causes you support, and the roles you choose. For example:

- Robert has always enjoyed leading complex projects. Over the years, he's devoted significant time to the various nonprofits he supports, taking charge of many of their major initiatives.
- Patty loved working with children. She was a Brownie leader, worked on school carnivals, invited kids to her house, and was the team mom for numerous sports teams.
- Jessica was detail-oriented from the time she was young. She loved organizing events and making sure that nothing fell through the cracks. She kept great records, too.

For me, coaching Odyssey of the Mind teams allowed me to tap into a creative side of myself that I'd never known before. I spent way more time volunteering than was necessary, but it was because it gave me joy.

Think of your favorite spare-time activities. What made you enjoy them so much? What was your contribution? What does that tell you about yourself?

What Kind of Person Do You Want to Be?

When you're hit by a pivotal moment, this is an interesting question to ask yourself. There are so many different options available to you—even though it might not seem like that at the time.

In *Atomic Habits*, author James Clear asks, "What do you want to stand for? What are your principles and values? What do you wish to become?"

Knowing what's important to you is crucial. It shapes your future choices and decisions—whether in your personal life, as part of a team, or in your community.

When I launched my What's Really Possible initiative, I made this pledge to myself and everyone else:

- I choose to think, live, and act in the spirit of possibility.
- I will bring my initiative, common sense, and decency to my family, community, country, and the world.
- I will work with others to find ways to solve the challenges we face and create the future we want.
- I commit to making a difference in thought, word, and deed in some way every day.
- I will do this with laughter, dedication, integrity, and love—because it's the right thing to do.

Doing this is a promise. To yourself. To others. It's about your relationships. Take some time to write about the person you want to be. It's a life-giving statement for your future. Of course, you won't become that person overnight, but you'll be heading in the right direction.

But Wait…There's More

While you're being introspective, here are a few other questions to think about:

- What Can You Do in Your Sleep?
  - This question points to a strength you might not even value because it's so second nature to you. My strength is that I can put myself into someone else's shoes and listen or react as if I were that person.
- What Bores You to Death?
  - You'll want to avoid this as you shape your future. Certain tasks may be tedious and necessary, but they shouldn't dominate your efforts. For me, this includes bookkeeping and accounting tasks.
- What Do You Suck At?
  - Look at the various jobs and roles you've had over the years. Knowing what you disliked doing is essential data. I suck when it comes to technology problems. They bring me to tears.

To sum it all up, you're unique. You have your strengths and your shortcomings. You have your aspirations and hopes.

The good thing is that the world needs people with all our different talents and interests. By looking inward, you'll make decisions that lead to your best possible future.

Chapter 8
Gaining Clarity

Amazingly, most of us know our limitations and weaknesses more than our strengths. Think about how often you compare yourself to others regarding your appearance, capabilities, status, smarts, and more.

Have you ever said, "Oh, I could never do that?" Was that true? In some situations, it might be. But in many cases, it's because we haven't had the opportunity or focused on that area. Sometimes, we let others define us with their blatant statements of who we are.

In college, I got a D in a technical writing class—my worst grade ever. Clearly, I couldn't have envisioned a future as an author. But about twenty years ago, I started writing one newsletter a month, then upped it to twice monthly. Next came a few how-to guides for my website.

I received positive feedback at every step of the way, which helped build my confidence. Twenty-five years ago, I could never have dreamed that I would publish five books and be invited to speak worldwide.

Do you ever stop to think about what you're really good at? Probably not too often. We're not always the best judges of ourselves. Sometimes, we need outside input to open our eyes to our top talents.

Exploring Your Impact

Years ago, I formed a women's group with four other friends. We planned to hold monthly dinner events featuring a speaker, conversation, and entertainment. Months before our September launch, we identified the topics we wanted speakers to discuss.

I was in charge of the October event and needed to find a woman who could talk about "power." I researched online, checked speakers' bureaus, and called my professional contacts. Zippo. Nada. I couldn't find a single woman who spoke about that topic.

At our next planning meeting, I admitted my failure. The next thing I knew, my so-called friends had assigned me the job of being the speaker for that night. I was horrified, but it was my responsibility. To make it even worse, I detested the topic—power. I didn't want power over anyone else. In fact, I'd pretty much spent my entire life avoiding it.

With my speech just a few weeks away, I called a good friend for help. I told Marci about my upcoming speech on power and how much I hated the topic. She said, "Jill, you've got it all wrong. Talk to your friends, your clients, and your family. Ask them, 'What impact do I have on you?'"

When I started asking, I was floored by what I discovered. People felt safe with me. I offered a calming presence in a storm. They wanted my optimistic thinking to help them connect with the positives in their lives. They said I inspired them to stop being complacent and to step up to their next level. They told me I helped them see possibilities and gave them the courage to move forward.

Then, it finally hit me what power was all about. My power and my impact were in my presence. I couldn't abdicate my power even if I wanted to. This new feeling of power felt honest, solid—like an internal strength. I also realized that using my voice, whether written or spoken, enabled me to have an even bigger, more positive impact on the world.

Finally, I knew I was ready to talk about real power. On the night of my speech, the emcee introduced me by saying, "Jill is a woman of power and influence. Please join me in welcoming her."

I walked to the front of the room, fully appreciating the applause and knowing I deserved every bit of it. Why? Because… I AM a woman of power and influence—and I always have been. But I would never have known that if I hadn't asked. It was just who I was. I already had strengths and I didn't even realize it.

This reminds me of *The Wizard of Oz*. The Scarecrow wanted a brain, the Tin Man wanted a heart, and the Cowardly Lion wanted courage. At the end, when Glinda granted each of them their wish in thanks for killing the Wicked Witch, she told them they already had the qualities they most desired. This might be you too!

I challenge you to ask your friends, family, and colleagues, "What impact do I have on you?" Faith Ralston, author of *Play Your Best Hand*, also has an assessment to determine team strength. And, to learn how your co-workers perceive what you excel at, she suggests asking, "What do you come to me for?" Again, this can be pretty revealing.

Finding Your Thriving Zone

Another helpful way to gain clarity about your strengths is to take one of the many available assessment tools. They can help you identify what you're good at, possible careers for someone with your talents, and the work environments where you will excel. Here's feedback from several I've taken:

- CliftonStrengths (formerly Gallop StrengthsFinder): According to this assessment, my top strengths are Learner, Maximizer, Activator, Ideation, and Self-Assurance. If I'd have known this earlier in my career, it might have given me more confidence in what I was doing.

- Myers-Briggs: The purpose of this assessment is to help people better understand themselves and others, which enables improved communication and better decisions. Personally, I'm an ENTP, which means that I'm extroverted, focused on possibilities, a thinker, and flexible.
- Enneagram: This assessment helps people understand their personality type and the unconscious patterns that drive their behavior. I'm a Seven, which means I'm curious, optimistic, and adventurous. I'm also future-oriented and like to get out there and make things happen.

It's good to know this information. It's data you might not perceive on your own, yet it can significantly impact your choices and satisfaction. It's also a validation of your unique gifts and talents. All of these assessments are available online too.

After seeing my results, can you imagine me in a job where maintaining the status quo was expected? I'd shrink, be a disruptor, and upset everyone around me. I've been there. I've also created relationship challenges because my ways of thinking, doing, and being differ significantly from those of others.

We all have different strengths and talents, and it's important to acknowledge that. But it all starts with knowing yourself.

> *He who knows others is wise.*
> *He who knows himself is enlightened.*
> —Lao Tzu

Chapter 9
Tapping Into Community

Experiencing a pivotal moment requires stepping into the unknown. Sometimes it's downright scary. You feel like you're the only one out there who's going through these challenges. You worry that you don't know enough. You question your ability to come out on the other side or to turn your idea into a reality.

During times of transition, you need support, guidance, answers, and hope. That's why engaging selected family, friends, and colleagues in your new adventure is so important. It's also vital to expand your network. Pivotal moments can take you into unknown territory.

Assemble Your Team

Different people bring you different gifts, so you'll want to think about who's on your team. Before you get discouraged, realize that you may not already know these people. But again, that's part of the adventure. If you're open to it, you'll meet them.

- Cheerleaders: These people believe in you, your talents, and your capabilities. They encourage you to keep on going, remind you of what you're good at, and know you can do it if you keep at it. Most of all, they want you to succeed. This moral support is invaluable.

- Inspirers: These people stimulate you mentally and invigorate you to take action. You'll feel a surge of energy and enthusiasm when you're with them. You'll want to live more fully, experience more joy, and create something new.
- Challengers: These people make you think—sometimes even when you don't want to. They'll question what you're doing and why. They'll invite you to consider alternate paths and strategies. But they do this because they want you to succeed.
- Butt-Kickers: If setting due dates and committing to them aren't your strength, having a friendly butt-kicker on your side can be a real asset. Sometimes you need an accountability partner.
- Experienced Pros: These people have already walked your path. Not only can they give you great advice, but they can also shorten your learning curve.

The good news is you don't have to know all of these people personally. Over the years, many authors have inspired and challenged me. They've shared invaluable lessons and insights that would have taken me ages to learn—if ever.

Plus, so much good information is available online—classes, videos, podcasts, forums, newsletters—the list could go on and on. Take advantage of these resources. But don't forget the people part. Not only is it helpful, but it's good for the soul.

Join or Create a Group

Being part of a group experience can also be valuable. By joining up with others, you discover you're not alone in facing a particular pivotal moment. You'll learn from the experiences of the other members, and you'll find that the emotional roller coaster you're on is something they've all faced.

Many groups today have a significant online presence where you can ask questions, find resources, and get the support you need. In-person meetings are essential, too, because that's where you'll get a feel for the greater community you're part of.

Over the years, I've created my own groups because I needed to be around people like me. With friends, I co-founded Awesome Women, a nonprofit focused on ensuring that "Every Woman's Voice Makes a Difference." I learned a lot—and together we helped others, too.

Then, I started a group for women sales experts. We'd get together annually to share ideas for growing our businesses, the best resources to use, and how to tackle various challenges. During the year, no matter what questions we had, there were people we could call for advice and encouragement.

I've also been part of a mastermind group at various points in my career. When I wanted to grow my speaking business, I met monthly with two others with the same goal. On our monthly phone calls, we shared what we were up to, brainstormed new ideas, and offered advice for dealing with our challenges. Finally, we'd make commitments to each other about what we'd get done by our next call. Knowing that we'd have to share our progress motivated us to get things done.

Become a Member

There's nothing like joining an association of people who share your interests. You can attend meetings and hear from expert speakers. You can connect with others who have deep knowledge in the areas you're focused on. You may even leave these events with pages of notes filled with new ideas and valuable resources.

Maybe even more importantly, you'll be with other human beings. That might be the best part. In between meetings, you connect with these people. You can brainstorm ideas. You can talk about challenges and get fresh perspectives.

And you'll develop invaluable relationships with these people that can last for years—or even decades.

Volunteer Your Time

Volunteering can offer so much. Whatever your interests, there's always someone or some group that could use a helping hand. More than anything, it can give you a sense of purpose, especially if you're at that in-between stage of your pivotal moment when you're unsure what to do next.

It can also provide an opportunity to learn new skills and gain valuable work experience. I spent ten years volunteering for groups that focused on creative problem-solving for students. I coached, judged, recruited, started a high school program, served on the state advisory board, and raised funds. Not only did I have lots of fun doing it, but I learned so much.

Today, I volunteer my time by writing a weekly newsletter focused on "Inspiring Positive Change in an Evolving World." I spend a lot of time on it because I want to make a difference.

Anyone who's been challenged by a pivotal moment needs people. Social connections matter—even if you're an introvert.

It's okay to ask for help and support. You're at a point of change in your life, walking down a new path to places you've never been. It can be hard. It can be exciting. But you don't have to go down that path alone.

But also consider who's giving you the advice. Do they truly have your best interests at heart? Are they responding to your request for assistance? Is their advice self-serving? Do they have the qualifications to make those recommendations?

Finally, ask yourself how the advice makes you feel. Do you feel supported, like they're trying to help you succeed? Or are they trashing your ideas?

Sometimes what you hear will scare you. That's normal. Your life is changing and you're moving into unknown territory.

Your community is invaluable. Use it!

Chapter 10
Envisioning Possibilities

Are you living on autopilot? If so, join the club. Most of us are. One day looks like the next, and one year turns into another. It's nice to have routines and to know what to expect, but could our lives be better? Could our relationships be deeper? Could our work be more fulfilling? If so, what would need to change?

Scary thoughts, right? Yet pivotal moments are a time for growth and rethinking. Imagine zooming out, exploring other possibilities, and then making changes to achieve your desired future.

To make the most of these pivotal moments, you have to kick yourself out of your comfort zone. It's tough, though. Our brains are designed to identify patterns and then systematize them. The bad news is that we're not actively learning new things or adjusting to changing conditions when we're on cruise control.

So, when we step outside our comfort zone, our brain screams at us, "Wrong way. Don't go there. It's not how we do things. You might fail." It's tough to change with messages like that swirling in our heads. It takes a conscious effort over time to live life differently.

Taking a Fresh Look

A fun way to start is to use the Odyssey Plan, developed by Stanford University and featured in the book *Designing Your Life*. It's not like the linear five-year plans that focus on your SMART goals, the steps you'll take to achieve them, and your timeframes.

Instead, the Odyssey Plan serves as an exercise in creative problem-solving. This thought experiment involves envisioning three different versions of yourself over the next five years. Creating these scenarios expands your mind to a broader range of ideas, ultimately leading to better decisions.

Also, there's no need to answer that "What's your passion?" question that stumps most of us. Research shows that only 20% of people can define their passion. The rest of us have to create our lives and continually assess whether we like the direction we're headed in.

To start, you'll need three unlined sheets of paper and something to write or draw with. You'll also need an attitude of fun and exploration. Remember, there are no wrong answers. Explore the three options below and consider where they might lead you.

- Plan #1: Map out your life if you stayed on your current path for the next five years. What job are you doing? What are your routines, relationships, and plans?
- Plan #2: Imagine your life if what you're doing today no longer exists. What will you be doing? What does this version of you end up like?
- Plan #3: Imagine a future where money and other people's opinions don't matter. What would you be doing? What would you create? How does it feel?

In other words, what do you want to be when you grow up? If you can identify what's important to you, you can start to figure out how to create that life.

Think about how much you like each plan. What appeals to you in each one? Can you bring some of the items you like in Plan #3 to other versions of yourself?

What questions would you have if you wanted to create a different reality from your current one? What resources would you need? What would it take to develop confidence in going in that direction? Finally, name that plan.

Evolving into the New You

As I've already said, I've reinvented myself multiple times. My dissatisfaction with my Teaching Era led me to my Salesperson Adventure. After trying different iterations, I entered my Consulting/Parenting Years. When I decided that I wanted to have a greater impact on small- and medium-sized businesses, I transitioned into the Speaker/Author Decade.

In all of these decisions, I took into account my evolving interests and motivations. My family life and desired lifestyle also played a big part. Then, I hit the Lost Era, where I was flailing around trying to figure out what to do next. We all go through that.

Today, I'm in the Fairy Godmother phase of my life. I want to share my hard-earned wisdom with others. And I want to tap them on the head with my magic wand to help them create new possibilities in their lives and for the world. That's my journey. But that's what life is all about—evolving, growing, learning, and expanding.

So, what does it take to find out your next step? Knowledge gathering. The best way to start is to go into learning mode. If you're looking at a particular career or job, interview people who are already doing that work. If you're interested in a healthcare career, consider the numerous options available to you.

Becoming a speaker was a big jump for me. I attended local association meetings to understand what makes good speakers effective in their presentations. I joined the National Speakers Association and attended regional and national conferences to gain a deeper understanding of the business aspects of this role. I visited numerous websites to see what others were doing. I started small, speaking to groups in the Minneapolis area and got better over time. It was a process.

You may also be considering lifestyle changes, which are fun to explore. Websites are filled with many resources. Talking to people who have "been there, done that" is invaluable. You can collect hints, valuable insights about what works, and so much more.

Starting on this journey can be challenging. It's not what you're used to. You're in unfamiliar territory. You're not even sure if you're asking the right questions. You're not sure what you need to do next. And, you may have doubts about your ability to succeed.

That's why it's important to remember that you're on an adventure! That's when the fun begins.

PART 3
Creating Your Future

Chapter 11
Designing Your Plan

A few years ago, I was asked, "Was your goal to be the number one women's sales expert in the world?" I laughed in shock. That was the farthest thing from my mind. I was just doing my work. Step by step, year by year, I kept moving forward without ever having that end goal in mind.

In the business world, many say that to achieve something you need SMART goals. That means they're Specific, Measurable, Achievable, Relevant, and Time-bound. However, SMART goals never worked for me during my transitional years. I had too much to learn and too many skills to develop. Even thinking about SMART goals was beyond my capabilities at the beginning of my journey.

That's why I love what Daniel Pink wrote in Drive, "The science shows that the secret to high performance isn't our biological drive or our reward-and-punishment drive, but our third drive—our deepest desire to direct our own lives, to expand and extend our capabilities, and to live a life of purpose."

So, it all starts with you! What are you interested in? What piques your curiosity? How can you make a difference for others?

What's important to you? These "why" goals will keep you motivated, even when times are tough.

Perhaps what matters to you is connected to your relationships. It may be related to lifestyle choices, health, education, or numerous other factors. And it needs to be taken into consideration with all the other factors.

Forward Momentum

Now, it's time to identify the decisions you need to make. Then step back and consider the pros and cons of each. Think about what might get in the way of a decision. It could be a wide range of factors.

When you decide to act on a pivotal moment, no matter what kind it is, you've entered the learning zone. The more you learn and the faster you learn, the closer you get to your next step. So, throw yourself into learning mode.

For example, if you want to start your own business, what kind would it be? What is your specialty? What will your organizational structure look like (Schedule C, Inc.)? Who else is in this field? How will your approach differ? Will you need to raise funds? If so, how will you do that? What are your plans for marketing? How will you implement them? I could continue on indefinitely.

When I put up my first website, I went into mega-learning mode. I identified dozens of people in essentially the same niche as mine. Then, I visited each of their websites. Before viewing them, I put on my prospective customer hat and asked myself, "Do they feel credible? Would I want to work with them? Do I have any concerns? Do I want to learn more about their services?"

After deconstructing what they were doing, I knew exactly what I wanted on my website. I wanted it to be a bit of fun. I wanted to create curiosity. I wanted it to be sticky, so people would read more instead of quickly moving on to a competitor's website. I also wanted to create valuable resources that visitors could freely download and share with others.

Yes, it took time. But it was the first step into my next phase, and I wanted to get it right. All that research and planning was well worth it, as it helped me visualize where I was going and obtain the right resources to make it possible.

But that was just the start. So much more was to come—much more than I could have even comprehended when I started on this journey. More than anything, at this point, you need the discipline to keep moving forward.

Next Steps

So what do you need to figure out? It helps to outline, to the best of your knowledge, specifically what actions you need to take to achieve your desired goal. It's best to take things one step at a time.

A while back, I heard an interview with Tiger Woods shortly after he'd won a few big tournaments following a three-year drought. The sportscaster asked him, "So, how do you think you're doing?" His response: "I'm getting better." He'd been focusing on various aspects of his golf game where he could improve.

For me, embarking on Jill's Urban Adventure required lots of next steps. First, I needed to prepare my house for sale. I began by discarding items that were no longer needed. Then, I consulted a realtor to determine what I could do to improve its value and help it sell quickly. Months later, I was ready to put it up for sale.

However, I still hadn't decided where I would live, so I had to educate myself on housing options in the downtown area. I visited numerous condos and townhomes in different neighborhoods. I needed to determine what factors mattered most to me. Decisions, decisions, decisions.

When I finally put my house on the market, it sold the first weekend. Then, I had to find a temporary place to live—and a place to store all my belongings. Six months later, I finally moved into my new place. But it needed some renovation too.

Any changes in our lives require us to think about and plan our next steps. It's like deciding to run a marathon. You don't just go out and run for twenty-six miles. Instead, you start small, running short distances. Then you run a little further. Once you're committed to the process, you begin to focus on other factors that could impact your performance.

Step by step, you get yourself to the starting line—and off you go! You'll never be perfect, but you don't have to be. Instead, you need to keep moving forward with minor ongoing improvements.

Get Going

The most effective way to achieve this is to commit to a plan that will help you reach your goal. Start thinking about all the things you need to put in place to create that forward motion.

Pick three things you can do to create forward momentum. Just three—otherwise, it gets overwhelming. Before you begin, take a moment to remind yourself of your "why" goals. They're the reason you're doing this.

As you look at each item, ask yourself, "What can I do today or this week to make progress?" Some items on your list may seem really boring. They're no-brainers that don't excite you one little bit. They just need to get done, so set a completion date. Then tell someone about it. Having accountability is an incentive for completion.

Other "to-dos" may seem overwhelming. They're so far beyond your current knowledge, skill level, or decision-making capability that you feel lost or discouraged. You don't have to make a giant leap forward. Instead, break down the larger tasks into smaller steps.

You don't have to know everything to start. You'll learn as you go. You'll discover strengths you didn't realize you had. And you'll get better, stronger, and more confident.

But what if it's not perfect? It likely won't be. You're in the learning phase. Plus, nothing is ever perfect. I'm still tweaking, updating, and refining projects I started years ago.

Make sure you keep congratulating yourself on the progress you're making. Don't wait till your end goal is achieved. Celebrate each step along the way.

Chapter 12
Reducing Gulp Moments

Not sure what to do next? Pivotal moments do that to you. You're in limbo. If you're like most of us, you've been living on autopilot. Moving into an unknown future can be downright scary. But it could also be the best thing you've ever done.

Even the smartest, most talented people have gulp moments, where they question their abilities—and maybe even their sanity. I can remember saying, "What in the world was I thinking when I decided to...?"

Reframing Failure

Over the years, I've failed often. Sometimes these were minor failures, but other times, they were whoppers. I'll never forget the rookie mistake I made when I started selling copiers. When I first spoke with Tinsey, the CEO's assistant, she told me that she made the final buying decisions.

But over the weekend, I read a book that stated I needed to talk with Mr. Big, not a lowly underling. On Monday morning, I called and set up a meeting with the CEO. When I arrived later that week, Tinsey came to the lobby to escort her boss's visitor up to his office.

She was shocked to see me standing there—and furious about what I'd done. She verbally attacked me with a vengeance. Four-letter words were flying. In shock, I fainted dead away onto the floor.

Did I fail? You betcha. After I was revived, Tinsey escorted me to the door and told me never to come back. I never did. When I got in my car, I burst into tears. I thought my career was over. I was humiliated.

That was a big pivotal moment for me. Still in shock, I spent the rest of the day trying to figure out what to do.

Ultimately, I chose to view that event as a beginner's mistake—an opportunity for growth. I asked myself, "What did I learn?" After reflecting on it, I realized that I would have been upset too if someone had gone behind my back. And then I thought of other ways I could have handled the situation better.

Everything changes when you reframe failures as "valuable learning experiences." You stop being so hard on yourself. You quit trying to do things perfectly. You're a whole lot less stressed, which is beneficial, as your brain can now think more clearly and creatively. It also frees you up to experiment and grow in your capabilities.

This mindset is crucial when you're doing something new. If you're still hung up on failing, you have a choice. You can live in fear of failure and become only a fraction of the person you're meant to be. Alternatively, you can reframe failure in a way that allows you to accept mistakes as just a natural part of learning.

Remember, if you're struggling, you're not failing. You just haven't figured it out yet. Not only does it reduce your gulp moments, but it also motivates you to keep going, knowing that success is imminent.

Sometimes, reframing failure is even more important when you're an experienced person. If it's been a long time since you've been in a learning mode, you're rusty at picking up new information. You'll feel awkward trying out new skills. Every bone in your body will want to revert to your habitual way of doing things.

Beating Imposter Syndrome

When I first started consulting, I was shocked when corporate executives took my advice seriously. After all, I was just me with my limited credentials. I thought I should know more, be smarter, and have a greater depth of experience. When I compared myself to the bigwigs, I often felt inadequate.

But the truth was that I was stretching myself in a new direction. Just because I was uncomfortable with my new role didn't mean I was incapable of handling it. To help me deal with these feelings, I had to remind myself that:

- I was in growth mode and was capable of learning new things.
- If these executives had confidence in me, I just might be better than I thought.
- If I got stuck, I could ask questions and seek guidance.

The truth is, imposter syndrome is just your brain saying, "OMG. You've never done this before. Abort. Abort. Go back to safety."

Fear. Uncertainty. Doubt. These emotions are mind games, not reality. Yes, they're scary. They can cripple your forward momentum if you let them. You need to remind yourself that they're not accurate statements of your capabilities. And truthfully, you'll never be ready enough.

Take time to remember what you're good at, too. You've had accomplishments that you're proud of. Celebrate the progress you've already made. Feel free to discuss your feelings with friends, colleagues, and family members. They're your cheering squad—and your advisors.

Pivotal moments are a time for growth and rethinking. Whether it's a professional challenge or a personal one, you need to keep moving forward.

Thinking Negatively

You've probably heard about the importance of positive thinking. For years, motivational gurus have encouraged us to visualize achieving our goals. It's so inspirational! So rah-rah.

However, thinking positively can backfire on you. Seriously. Research by Dr. Gabriele Oettingen, a psychologist at New York University, says that the better you are at visualizing your goals, the less likely you are to achieve them. That's a shocker—and so opposite of what the gurus are telling you.

What happens is that visualization causes your brain to relax; it thinks the hard work has already been done. As a result, you lose focus and clarity, making it much harder to reach your goals.

Instead, Dr. Oettingen discovered that "mental contrasting" is far more effective than positive thinking alone. Essentially, that means that you're visualizing two things at once:

1. How great it will be to (fill in your goal).
2. All the obstacles that stand in the way of achieving that goal.

Identifying the obstacles is crucial to your success. Take time to think about what could go wrong. Review your plan to determine what's missing. Take a stab at what mistakes you might inadvertently make.

You may also want to consult with others who have followed a similar path. Ask them, "What am I missing? What obstacles did you encounter? What didn't you anticipate?" Then, figure out how you might deal with these potential negative situations.

The incredible power of negative thinking prevents epic failures. And when combined with the great feeling you'll experience upon accomplishing your goal, you'll be ready to tackle the tasks and activities necessary to maximize success.

Failure is your route to success. If you don't choose to learn from your mistakes, you're doomed to repeat them again and again, until you either quit or finally get it. But once you reframe failure as a chance to learn, you move forward. That's why this mindset matters.

Chapter 13
Getting More "AHAs"

Turning your pivotal moment into a life-enhancing event can be a real stretch for most of us. It's not something we do every day. That means we may need some new approaches to trigger our thinking and shift our perspectives.

Sometimes we don't know enough or, worse yet, don't even know what we don't know. We're neophytes who lack the knowledge and skills to handle challenging situations or to take us to the next level. That's when things can get tough for us, especially if we're on our own.

Borrow a Brain

Early in my career, I encountered a strategy that has provided significant dividends for me over the years. To learn the ropes, each new hire was assigned to work with a top-notch salesperson for a few months. Jim was my guy. He was masterful. I hoped that someday I could achieve his level of competence.

When I finally got my own territory, I was scared. I remember sitting in my car outside an office building, terrified to go in. My mind was racing through various challenging scenarios. What if the customer asked me about our new product and I didn't know the answer? What if they said they weren't interested? What if, what if, what if...?

I was deep into catastrophizing when it hit me. I might not know how to respond, but Jim sure would. By thinking about how he'd react and using that as my guide, I could handle almost anything. From then on, when people asked questions I couldn't answer, instead of sounding like a babbling idiot, I parroted Jim, "Great question. Why is that important to you?"

"Borrowing" Jim's brain was a lifesaver for me. It allowed me to shift my perspective away from the angst that had paralyzed my thinking. Plus, it turned my problem into a question: "How would Jim handle this?" Suddenly, my brain had an irresistible challenge to solve and immediately went to work. New ideas and answers quickly came to mind, enabling me to handle the numerous scenarios I had feared.

Over the years, I've done a lot of "brain borrowing." It's a creative problem-solving approach used by innovative companies to shift perspective. Hillary Clinton employed this strategy when she transitioned to her new role as First Lady. She'd constantly ask herself, "What would Eleanor Roosevelt do?"

Next time you're stumped, consider borrowing someone else's brain. It's a perfect strategy to use when you're developing the necessary confidence, knowledge, and skills to deal with unfamiliar or uncomfortable situations. Use it when you need fresh perspectives as well. Don't let your own limited experience trap you.

Create Challenges

Over the years, I've traveled on a few bumpy roads in my profession. I'll never forget the day I was debriefing a project with Bill, one of my major clients. As I left, he said, "Give me a call next week and we'll get going on the next phase." I assured him I would.

As promised, I reached out to him and left a message. He didn't call back. I emailed him, but I got no response. I tried calling and emailing repeatedly. Nothing. Finally, after a month, I sent him a message that said, "I'm so sorry, Bill. I must have done something to offend you. Please accept my apologies."

Minutes later, he called me back and apologized for his lack of response. It wasn't me who was the problem. It was him. He had way too much to do and not enough time to accomplish it. He was totally frazzled.

That was the day it hit me. Everyone was crazy-busy. The old ways of doing business were a thing of the past. Totally gone. And it was a real problem for people in my profession. We couldn't set up meetings. Plus, getting prospective customers to change from the status quo required too much time and effort for them.

For months, I moaned and groaned about the situation. But one day, a light bulb went off. I realized that viewing my situation as a problem was sapping my creative energy. Even when well-intentioned friends offered good ideas, I was pessimistic and dismissive.

I was caught in a downward spiral of negativity. Just when I needed all the brainpower I could muster, it was unavailable to me.

Everything changed when I turned my problem into a challenge. I said to myself, "Jill, this is a challenge. You don't know the solution, but you're good at solving puzzles. You can figure this out."

When I did that, a few things happened immediately. I regained a sense of control over my future, and my brain started working again. I became curious and began experimenting with different approaches. Ultimately, I discovered far more effective ways of working—which led me to write *SNAP Selling: Speed up Sales and Win More Business with Today's Frazzled Customers*.

My experience isn't unique. Neuroscience research shows that when you make a mental shift to view obstacles as opportunities, your brain is reenergized. It loves challenges and immediately starts scanning the environment, looking for insights that may be helpful to you. It also starts digging into your past, looking for previous experiences you've had that might be helpful.

Suddenly, you find relevant information that you overlooked when you were wallowing in the mud. Maybe you'll be reading an article that's not even relevant to your specific challenge, but it triggers a new idea. Or you'll wake up with a fresh perspective on how to address a difficult situation. Good ideas seem to appear out of nowhere when your brain is in this state.

For most people, creating challenges out of problems is not a natural habit. However, as I've discovered, this mindset frees up your creative energy, enabling you to devise unique solutions that yield significantly better results.

Ask Different Questions

Sometimes your desired future seems unattainable. You look at what's happening in your life, your career, and your world, and it overwhelms you. You might ask, "What can I do about it?" But, as a singular person, you don't feel like you have nearly enough expertise or power even to make a dent. So, you do nothing.

Over the years, I've found that certain types of questions can spark creativity and provide you with more ideas than you initially imagined.

For example, at one point in my life, I was particularly interested in working with small companies. Not only are they more innovative than large corporations, but they're also more concerned about their local community. And that's where the job growth was happening.

But money was always tight. It was a big issue. Rather than walking away from them, I asked myself this question: "How can I help these small businesses that can't afford me?"

I started thinking about it. I wrote a few e-books and posted them on my website as free downloads. I freely shared other people's content via my newsletter. I did online presentations.

The next question I asked was: "How can I share my expertise for free and still earn a good income doing it?" I thought it was a crazy question, but before long, an answer appeared. A big company had seen my free e-books and asked if I could write one for them.

When I said yes, they wanted to know how much I'd charge. We agreed on a tidy sum. Additionally, we agreed that they would make it available for free forever and that after six months, I could share it on my website. This blossomed into a profitable business—and expanded to include webinars.

Then a recession hit, and many people lost their jobs—including my brother. That's when I asked, "How can I help all those people who lost their jobs through no fault of their own get back to work faster?" After thinking about it, I realized I could write a book on the topic—and give it away for free, which I did on the new website I created especially for job seekers.

Then I decided to do a series of webinars featuring experts who could help the jobless. So, I approached GoToMeeting to see if they'd let me use their platform for free. They said they didn't do that. So, I asked, "What do you do?" They said they paid for "butts in seats," meaning I'd get paid a small amount for each attendee. In addition to my normal work, I did that for eighteen months and helped many people in the process.

When I worked with nonprofits, I asked these types of questions: "How can we collaborate with our competitors and amplify our impact?" or "How can we help women realize just how much the world needs their voices?"

Today, I'm asking, "How can I inspire positive change in an evolving world?" I don't know the answer, but I know it's the journey I'm on these days, and I'm learning from it.

Throw away those "Can I?" questions. Instead, ask "How" questions. They're provocative. They'll get you thinking. They'll open up new possibilities for you…because in reality, so much more is possible than we can even imagine.

> *I not only use all the brains I have, but also all that I can borrow.*
>
> —President Woodrow Wilson

Chapter 14
Dancing with Discouragement

Pivotal moments can be downright challenging. You may be forced to make decisions you never wanted to make. The road you've chosen could be bumpier than you expected. You've tried hard to move forward, but nothing seems to be working. You start feeling bummed out. Then fear starts seeping in.

You may be nodding your head right now, saying, "That's my situation exactly. It's sink or swim here—and right now, I'm sinking." It takes courage to make these changes in your life. You need to be tenacious and persistent, even in the face of insurmountable challenges.

This resilience is what University of Pennsylvania psychology professor Angela Duckworth calls "grit." According to her research, grit is a greater predictor of success than a person's innate intelligence or talents.

In the previous chapter, we focused on numerous strategies that can make a significant difference. Here are some additional ideas:

- **Take a break.** When you're under intense pressure and stressed out, your stick-to-itiveness quickly evaporates. It's time to give yourself a breather. When I feel that way, the best thing I can do is to move. For me, taking a walk burns off a lot of angst. And, when that happens, it opens my mind to fresh thinking.

- **Connect with others**. Talk with family, friends, and colleagues who are supportive of what you're doing. Share your feelings, ask questions, laugh, and have fun too. Knowing that others support you makes a huge difference. Plus, anything you do to take the pressure off, even momentarily, can renew your spirit.

- **Focus on what's controllable.** What's important from the start is to separate the areas you can influence from those you can't. Then, you need to consciously decide not to waste any of your valuable time on things you can't change. Instead, direct all your energy towards areas where you can have a positive impact, such as your skill level, depth of knowledge, time management, and mindset.

- **Avoid detrimental comparisons**. Whenever I've started something new, I find myself comparing my progress to those who are far ahead of me in that area. It doesn't help! Instead, what makes a difference is to talk with people who are one step ahead of you. Find out what they're doing and learn from their experiences. Not only does it shorten your learning curve, but it also makes you feel that your success is truly possible.

- **Create a fallback strategy**. Knowing that your world won't fall apart if things don't happen according to your timeline is about safety for you and your family. When I started in sales, I figured I could always fall back on waitressing to bring in some revenue. There have also been times in my career when I cut way back on unnecessary spending. Having significant credit card debt would only have exacerbated my angst.

- **Expand your options**. Years later, my consulting business was completely wiped out due to economic factors. At that time, I was willing to explore a much wider range of options, including returning to a sales job or assisting non-profits with their fundraising efforts. Sometimes you just need to get your mojo back—and that's a good enough reason for going sideways for a while.

- **Challenge your thinking**. If things aren't improving, you may need to shift into learning mode. Maybe you need to improve your interview skills. Perhaps you need to learn more about a particular industry. It could be a gazillion things you could re-evaluate. Be open to that. Get advice from others. It may be just what you need.

Most of all, don't give up on yourself. Developing grit makes a huge difference—not only to your success in your job today, but for your whole life.

Picker Uppers

Sometimes it's tough to motivate yourself to keep going. Sometimes you're just plain scared, unsure if you have what it takes to succeed. All you know is that you've had a pivotal moment that's sent you in this direction, and it's more challenging than you thought.

The first day I had to make a sales call all by myself, I was terrified. I sat in the car for a long, long while. Suddenly, a song that I'd heard as a kid popped into my head:

> Whenever I feel afraid
> I hold my head erect
> And whistle a happy tune
> So no one will suspect I'm afraid.
>
> While shivering in my shoes
> I strike a careless pose
> And whistle a happy tune
> And no one ever knows I'm afraid.
>
> The result of this deception
> Is very strange to tell
> For when I fool the people
> I fear I fool myself as well.

I started singing it. I held my head erect. I struck a careless pose. And, amazingly, like the song says, I fooled myself as well. I walked into that business feeling and acting like a professional.

Today, I have other songs that lift my spirits and keep me moving forward. I love "The Impossible Dream" and "I Hope You Dance." To get my mojo back, "Girl on Fire" is my newest favorite.

Quotes can be impactful too. I still have one that a man handed me decades ago at a professional meeting. I thought it was his business card. Instead, it was a quote from Robert Schuller: "Never believe in Never." As someone who focuses on what's possible, it warms my heart and keeps me motivated.

***

Don't let setbacks define who you are. They're just part of your journey into the next phase of your life. Yes, they're tough. But they can be overcome. You can do it!

Chapter 15
Enjoying Serendipity

Over the years, I've discovered that when I'm on the right path, the universe seems to be there helping me out. You could say I'm lucky. But it's more than that. I truly believe that if you've done enough preparatory work to get you started in a new direction, amazing things can happen. Here are a few examples:

Leaving Teaching

Earlier, I described how I'd hit the wall as a teacher, and no one would hire me. That pissed me off enough that I decided to start my own company. I spent months researching, thinking, planning, and creating a business plan. When the SCORE consultant informed me that "someone had to sell it," I reluctantly agreed.

I'll never forget the day I attended the job fair at the St. Paul Civic Center. Many big companies were going to be there, so I was hopeful. I called in sick that morning. It turned out I was such a nervous wreck that I almost stayed home. But I couldn't waste a good sick day, so I ended up arriving around 11:30. Within an hour, I'd been rejected by all the companies where I thought I might have a chance, so I decided to leave.

As I was walking down the large ramp to the parking lot, there was just one man walking up the ramp. He asked me what I thought of the job fair. I told him about my experience. He said, "Did you talk to the people at Xerox?" When I said I hadn't, he said, "Come with me. I'm the guy who organized this whole event, and this shouldn't be happening."

A few minutes later, we were at the Xerox booth. He introduced me to the main guy there and said, "You need to hire her. She's good." The next week, I was called to set up some interviews and to take an aptitude test. One month later, I started my new career.

Changing My Focus

I was in my early forties and bored with my work. My clients saw me as simply a vendor for hire. What I really wanted to do was more strategic work where I could significantly impact their success. Unfortunately, no one I worked with saw me that way—including me!

People who did strategic work had MBAs. They'd worked at big-name consulting firms. They had a track record of delivering impressive results. My background was teaching and sales, which was clearly insufficient for credibility. I decided I needed to get a master's degree.

I researched all the colleges near me to find the right program. I studied hard for the GMAT test, a prerequisite for admission. I was ecstatic when I passed. The first class I took was Public Speaking. Since I'd been a teacher and trainer, I figured it'd be the easiest way to get back into student mode—and earn a good grade.

Midway through the class, one of my clients called to talk about a project he wanted me to do. When I met with him, he asked me to work on a strategic initiative. I was stunned. From my perspective, I wasn't qualified, yet he wanted me on the project.

Soon after that, another client contacted me. They wanted me to be involved in future scenario planning sessions they were putting on for their customers. When I said I'd never done anything like that before, they told me I'd be working as their representative with the Boston Consulting Group—and I'd learn everything I needed to know.

Just like that, my business shifted. I knew what direction I wanted to take. I completed the work required to gain admission to the master's program and was taking my first class. I never took another one. It wasn't necessary.

Landing a Book Contract

After all I'd learned about setting up meetings with corporate executives, I decided to write the book *Selling to Big Companies*. I'd just about finished writing the proposal, but wasn't sure what to do next. I wanted a decent publisher and hoped to find an agent. That was a big ask for a first-time author with no established track record of success.

That's when I got an email from a consultant I'd met a few years earlier. At the end, his signature file read, "Author of ROI Selling." I sent him a "Big Congrats!" note. Moments later, he called me. We talked about his book, his excitement, his publishing process, and more.

And then he asked, "Have you ever thought about writing a book?" "Yes," I answered. "I'm just about done with my proposal." He asked me what it was going to be about. I shared my concept. As we were about to hang up, he said, "I just sent a quick note to my publisher. He's interested in seeing your proposal as soon as it's ready." I was in shock. It all happened so fast. I wasn't quite ready, but I asked him to make the introduction via email.

It took me a few weeks to polish off my proposal. When I was done, I researched other publishers I wanted to consider my book. Then I found the correct contact info and sent an email saying, "I've just finished a book proposal. XXX publisher is interested in seeing it. I wonder if you'd like to review it too."

Of course, they didn't want to pass on something another publisher deemed worthy. Within a few days, I had secured three interested publishers. At that point, I contacted an agent and told him, "I have three publishers wanting to see my proposal. I need someone to negotiate terms." Within a week, he was working for me. And less than two months later—and one very serendipitous connection—I was on my way to becoming an author.

The Right Path

Amazing things can happen when we're on the right path in life. When we're not, things come to a halt. Opportunities don't arise, you don't meet the right people, and you don't get new ideas.

Sometimes, it takes a while to figure that out. However, I can guarantee that you'll make new connections when you start taking the necessary steps to create your post-pivotal moment life. It could be an individual who shares invaluable advice with you, a resource that you really need at that moment in time, or a next step that you'd never considered before.

Just do the work and keep your eyes open for serendipity to happen to you. But don't take it for granted. Remember, serendipity is an opportunity... a door opening. It doesn't guarantee success. You still have to work hard, be creative, and deliver the goods.

And, if your serendipitous opportunity doesn't turn out to be what you'd hoped for, it's still a chance to learn invaluable lessons. Ultimately, it'll lead you to creating more possibilities and success in your next adventure.

Chapter 16
Blazing a New Trail

Pivotal moments jolt you out of your comfort zone. They send you on an adventure you never intended to take. Most of all, they serve as a springboard to new possibilities in your life, your career, your family, and more.

By embracing these pivotal moments, you'll discover what you're capable of. You'll focus on what matters to you.

Yes, it can be scary. It can take longer than you want to create this new reality. And, like everyone, at times you'll be discouraged. But keep on going. Creating a new and better future is well worth the effort.

Here's a good question to ask yourself: What have you said yes to that created other possibilities?

I remember when I got so frustrated that all the experts in my field were bald white men. Not that I have anything against them; it's just that I needed to see people like me who were successful. I contacted some women authors, but they weren't interested in stepping up.

That's when I realized I had to be the person who acted. I started by compiling a list of women sales experts I'd discovered online and noted their specialties. I contacted organizations that held sales and marketing conferences to express concerns about their lack of female speakers. When they said they didn't know any, I'd refer them to several options.

Not only did this highlight top women professionals in my niche, but it also helped me. That was a surprise, as it was never my intention. I started speaking more. I developed friendships with some incredibly talented women. We formed a mastermind group, helping one another grow. That was twenty-plus years ago.

Every new challenge you take on stretches you. It increases your confidence and your self-worth. It connects you with new people and new opportunities. You will be in the midst of an upward spiral—and that's a wonderful place to be!

Remember, you don't have to know all the details when you start. You will make mistakes—perhaps even foolish ones. But you will be able to figure it out with the help of your family, friends, and colleagues.

Make sure you know what difference you're trying to make. Focus on the positive impact your efforts can have on your life, family, community, colleagues, and others.

PART 4
Inspiring Action

Pivotal Moment Stories

This past year, I've talked with many people about the pivotal moments in their lives. Friends, colleagues, acquaintances, and even strangers willingly shared their stories. Many are quite successful today, but it wasn't always that way.

We've talked about what they went through, the challenges they faced, the decisions they made, and the actions they took. Ultimately, their pivotal moment had a positive impact on their lives. I'm so grateful they've agreed to share their stories.

In the upcoming chapters, you'll find stories about how these people were able to:

- Find unstoppable ideas
- Gain new perspectives
- Embrace opportunities they encountered
- Get unstuck and move forward
- Find fullness in their lives.

May their pivotal moments be the springboard to new possibilities in your life!

Chapter 17
Finding Unstoppable Ideas

It's incredible how some of the worst possible things we encounter can morph into a life-changing opportunity for us. Without the challenge we faced, we would have never gone on this journey.

When No Became My Starting Point

He said it so casually that it almost didn't register at first.

"Don't bother continuing. You're no good at this sport. And I don't have time to teach or coach you."

We were outside after the basketball game. My mom's older brother, our family chief, had come because I asked him. He mattered. His approval mattered. That day, I'd played through pain, jammed fingers, and the nerves of having him there, hoping for a slight nod of encouragement.

Instead, I got a sentence that felt like a door closing. It was summer 2006.

I walked home in silence, my hands still sore and stiff, my body aching. When I arrived, I told my mom what he'd said. She listened. She didn't try to spin it or make it better. She just gave me the space to decide what that moment was going to mean.

And that's when I knew. That was when I decided to prove him wrong. Not just him. Every voice that ever hinted I couldn't. Every doctor who said I should avoid physical activity. Every adult who assumed my height meant I should play, but my gender meant I wouldn't go far. I didn't know what "far" looked like yet. But I knew I was going.

That moment wasn't dramatic. There was no music, no applause, no spotlight. Just me, in a small room, deciding to go all in.

Only months earlier, in June 2005, I'd woken up in the elevator of L'Hôpital Général de Douala after undergoing an open tibial bone biopsy. The doctors couldn't explain what they'd seen on my X-ray, so they needed to find out.

The tumor was benign, but the aftermath of that procedure came with a warning that changed everything: no sports, no strenuous physical activity, play it safe. For most of my childhood, I'd been in and out of hospitals; sickness was my normal. Still, that sentence took me by surprise.

So, I chose basketball and joined a basketball academy in November 2005. Not because it was safe, but because it wasn't. Because I was tall. Because my friends played. Because my uncles had played. Because I wanted to see what I could become if I refused to listen to fear, or even to well-intentioned advice.

I practiced as hard as I could. I stayed after team drills to work on my shot. I ran extra laps. My mom woke me at dawn for conditioning. I studied the game. I paid attention to my coaches. Whenever I felt doubt creeping in, I reminded myself of that day. That sentence. That silence. That decision.

Months later, I joined an amateur team. Then I was invited to a basketball camp that changed the direction of my life. I outworked everyone because I carried more than just ambition. I carried a promise I'd made to myself.

From there, I was invited to the national team tryouts and made the roster. I trained harder, pushed further, and earned my spot on the squad that would represent Cameroon internationally. That visibility eventually opened the door to something even bigger—a scholarship to study and play basketball in the United States.

That one week in 2007 became a springboard. My life before was full of potential but shaped by limitations: medical warnings, family expectations, and a culture where girls didn't always get the same shot. After that moment, I saw possibilities. I saw a future I could shape on my own terms.

That decision is why I landed in the United States in 2010. It's why I was able to lead my college team to its first league championship and NCAA tournament bid. It's why I kept pushing through injuries, doubt, and unfamiliar territory.

My life didn't change because someone opened a door for me. It changed because someone closed one. And I chose to build my own.

ANGELA BOTIBA, originally from Cameroon, Central Africa, is a health care professional in Minneapolis. She holds an MHA/MBA from the University of Minnesota and works in Corporate Finance at Fairview Health Services.

Shifting Gears

The first day of radiation treatment was one of the hardest days of my life.

I had done everything I could to mentally and emotionally prepare, but I still wondered: "How on earth am I going to get through this?"

I knew I had to call on my inner warrior. So, I crafted my own Wonder Woman uniform: a red T-shirt with the yellow logo and a royal-blue tutu covered in stars. If I was going to face this head-on, I was going in armed. I was determined to kick Bubba's ass to the curb and show the world—and myself—what I was made of.

Bubba, as I named the uninvited guest lodged at the base of my brain between my eyeballs, came with an entourage: a rare and relentless disease called acromegaly. It wreaked havoc on nearly every aspect of my being—physically, mentally, and emotionally.

This was my new reality. But Bubba would soon become a very present voice in my life—and eventually, a cheerleader, a comedian, and an insightful guide.

After wrapping up my treatment, I found myself confined to the sofa and a pair of tattered gray sweatpants. This is no way to live, I thought. I needed something to strive for. A goal. Something just for me.

That's when I decided I would ride my bike from Canada to Mexico, down the Pacific Coast.

The logistics were overwhelming. I had no idea how my body would respond to a 1,845-mile journey. But I wanted to do this. I had to do this. And I had fourteen months to figure out how to get off that sofa and get myself to the US/Canadian border.

After months of building my strength and endurance, and weeks into my bicycle journey, I found myself somewhere near Big Sur, pedaling at 3 mph into gale-force winds. My legs were burning, but my heart cracked wide open. I looked out over the cliffs and realized I was no longer fighting for my life… I was living it.

I completed the ride in forty-one days, with only four rest days; I even wrote a book about it. To be honest, making it to the US/Mexican border felt anticlimactic. The road had tested me in ways I never imagined—but also showed me what was possible. I realized my road didn't end there. It kept going. And it was up to me to pave my own way.

From that point on, it became clear: most of my doubts, worries, and fears were often self-imposed, keeping me from having a much roomier perspective. That ride didn't just change me—it unleashed me, launching me into a more expansive mindset and an inspired life.

Pivotal moments don't always come with warning signs. Sometimes they knock us completely sideways.

But how we move forward from there—and whether we stay open to possibility—is what can propel us forward.

We all have unlit sparks. Bucket list dreams we keep postponing. Personal visions gathering dust.

But life happens. We run into roadblocks—and sometimes get completely blindsided.

***

Still, you have the power to pivot.
To unleash yourself from self-imposed constraints.
To (re)pave your own road.
Starting now.

RISA AUGUST is an award-winning author, speaker, and Gestalt practitioner who inspires intentional transformation. She dares others to dismantle limiting beliefs, shift their mindset, and step boldly into a life fully unleashed.

My Mess Became My Ministry

Every entrepreneur has a defining moment when they're forced to stop, reflect, and decide whether to give up or level up. For me, it came when I least expected it—flat on my back, on bed rest, facing the very real possibility of losing everything I'd built.

In the early 2000s, I'd built the largest woman-owned video production company in Philadelphia. My then-husband had joined our business full-time. By all outward appearances, we were thriving.

But the truth was far more complicated. I was the CEO, the chief rainmaker, and, frankly, the bottleneck to getting things done. If I wasn't there, business stalled. And like many entrepreneurs, I wore my exhaustion like a badge of honor.

Then came my pregnancy with JoJo—a miracle, but one with complications. It was a high-risk pregnancy, and I was ordered to complete six months of bed rest. All I could do was pray that he'd be fine.

Back then, I couldn't run my business from home (there was no Wi-Fi). My world basically came to a screeching halt. For the first time ever, I had to sit with the silence of my thoughts. Without the distraction of work, I confronted some hard truths. My business was in chaos, my marriage was struggling, and the health of my baby was uncertain.

I was a hostage to my own success. What saved me during that dark period was an old yellow legal notepad. I started writing down every lesson I'd learned in my business—the mistakes, the missed opportunities, and especially the expensive lessons.

When I finally put down the pen, I'd created a blueprint of what I wished someone had told me when I started out. I realized that no one was out there sharing practical everyday small business advice in the media.

When I noticed a gap in the marketplace, I wondered if I was the one to fill it. I talked to my pastor. His simple advice was to start praying about it. For months, I asked God, "What am I supposed to do next?" The answer came to me in a dream three times: "Become America's #1 small business expert."

At first, I doubted this calling. Who was I to take this on? But God doesn't call the qualified; He qualifies the called. So, I began studying people who'd become experts. They had books, media exposure, consistent branding, and lots of educational content.

My first step was to get a book deal—which I did. I transformed that yellow notepad into my bestseller, *Become Your Own Boss in 12 Months*. But just as I was preparing to share my book with the world, the Great Recession hit, and my publisher shelved it for eighteen months. I was devastated.

Fortunately, God had another plan. During that delay, I got started on Twitter and became the SmallBizLady. I posted helpful small business articles daily. I launched a blog, started an online chat, and ultimately, a weekly podcast.

When the book was finally published, it became one of the definitive guides to starting a business. At last, I was helping entrepreneurs design businesses that supported their dreams rather than leading them to overwhelm and financial ruin.

I also kept giving away free practical advice through my content hubs because I remembered what it was like to feel alone and unsure when I reinvented my business.

That forced bed rest was the greatest gift of my life. It gave me the space to listen to God's calling instead of my ego. I learned that my mess could become my ministry and that relentless consistency, visibility, and humility are the formula for long-term success.

I'll never forget where it started: with a yellow notepad, in my bed, with a prayer for direction.

MELINDA EMERSON, SmallBizLady, is America's #1 Small Business Expert. She's a bestselling author, keynote speaker, and CEO on a mission to end small business failure and empower entrepreneurs worldwide.

Tithing My Time

In 2006, Dave Breen, one of my closest friends and also my business partner, died suddenly. It hit me hard. Really hard. After coming up for air a few years later, I was looking to make a tangible difference in the lives of others, just like Dave had done throughout his lifetime.

I'd always been good at writing checks to charitable organizations, but I hadn't done anything that "inconvenienced" me. Nor had I dedicated any serious time to things outside my family and work. I volunteered at church and worked on other small projects, but none required much time.

That's when I came across a YouTube video from Francis Chan. In it, he explains what a gymnast does on a balance beam and how, when they're finished, they dismount, receive applause, and are then judged on their performance.

Chan then related the gymnast to our relationship with God and how often we try to live the safest life possible. We do whatever it takes NOT to be inconvenienced by others, yet we still expect His blessing. Finally, he challenges us to do something with our lives.

This video rocked me. I was the gymnast wanting all the accolades but unwilling to sacrifice time and work.

***

At almost the same time that I saw this video, Brian, another close friend of mine, had gone on a mission trip to Mexico to build a home for a family. I wanted to learn more about his trip. When

Brian explained his experience, I knew right away I had to challenge myself with this.

But going to a foreign place with no running water and scarce electricity, interacting with people who don't speak my language, and staying at a mission base in a room with several other guys was not one bit what I was used to. Talk about getting me out of my comfort zone!

Finally, in 2012, I went to Ensenada, Mexico with Brian and ten others. Our job? Working through Homes of Hope to build one home for a hard-working family who truly needed it.

This was my balance beam moment. I looked forward to seeing where God would lead me next, but I had no idea what He had in store.

***

Long story short, I've just returned from my fifteenth trip to Mexico. Thanks to that simple yes (and God doing the rest), we've taken over 1,500 volunteers on our mission trips. They come from all over the US and range from as young as eight to as wise as eighty.

Better yet, we've raised enough money to build 104 homes (and counting!) for people experiencing homelessness.

We also visited and supported a local orphanage and a women's shelter. We've also supported the missionaries who serve alongside us. They've surrendered everything in their life to help people experiencing poverty.

I once heard a quote that being a Christian is not jumping on a cruise ship but rather jumping into a rowboat and grabbing your oar every day. It's so true and so rewarding. My relationship with God does not just involve doing things; the fruit of that relationship has evolved into sacrificing for others whenever possible.

We often talk about tithing our income, which involves giving 10% to charity. I've come to believe that tithing your time is just as essential and is needed now more than ever.

It's still easy for me to write a check—and I do that with much joy—but it's a real game-changer when I can get involved and do the work.

TODD JOHNSON is a Certified Financial Planner (CFP®) with Provision Financial Group, a private wealth advisory practice through Ameriprise Financial, specializing in helping clients enhance their life and their legacy.

The Silver Lining to Getting Sacked

I didn't plan to start my own business so soon. But then I was fired. Yep, just like that, my manager gave me the news. I'd recently lost a big deal to a competitor, but I didn't expect to be fired. I left the office, went home, and took my dog for a hike. Sure, I shed a few tears, but there was really nothing I could do to change the situation.

In hindsight, this was good news. I'd been thinking about starting my own company, and many people encouraged me. This was in 1996, and the economy was robust. Of course, the silver lining wasn't immediately apparent. In the beginning, I felt rejected and worried about the sudden loss of income.

My initial goal was to work with small-to-medium companies to craft their growth strategy. I had worked with enough of these firms to know that, while they all had a business plan, you couldn't find a section on business development if you tripped on it.

My first client, a referral, was on the leadership team at an outplacement firm. By chance, they were conducting a customer satisfaction survey with fifty of their best clients. The survey was conducted in several rounds. On the last one, I added a question, "Would you be willing to offer a referral to this client?"

***

To this day, I have no idea where the question came from. The survey had a seven-point scale, with seven being the highest. The average response to my question was 6.5. And, better yet, fifty of this company's best clients said they'd be glad to give referrals.

Was this company asking for them? Nope. But that survey was the genesis of what would become my new business. My wheels began to turn. As I reflected on my career, I realized my best business had come from referrals.

While it had never crossed my mind that I'd launch a referral business, I was now focused on validating my beliefs. I conducted my on-the-ground research and interviewed sales leaders and salespeople. I asked specific questions about referrals. Here's how it went:

- Do you like to get referrals? (It seems like a dumb question, because everyone likes them, but I had to ask.)
  - The Answer: Absolutely.
- Do you have a referral system, a methodology, or a programmatic written strategy with metrics, KPIs, skills, and accountability for results?
  - The Answer: No. And, to this day, the answer is still no.

That was the pivotal question. Now I'm a logical person. So, I had to figure out why everyone said referral business was the best business, but no one had a referral system in place.

Thus, No More Cold Calling was born. I saw the opportunity. I did my research. And then I went into creator mode, focused on the one crucial skill that could positively impact so many people.

When I reflect on my career, I realize that referrals have always been my secret to success. In fact, my first job out of college was a referral. My uncle knew someone and introduced me. I was referred to both consulting firms I worked for, and my first client was a referral. I've always said that referrals work whether you're looking for a job, looking for a client, or looking for a date.

I say this, not just because referrals are my business, but because a lifetime of experience has proven to be true.

As you consider what to do with your pivotal moment, take some time to think about how you might leverage referrals. It could make a big difference!

JOANNE BLACK is America's referral authority, author of two books, and creator of the proprietary Referral Selling System. Referrals drive revenue, secure one-call meetings, and have a close rate of over seventy percent.

Finding My "No-Fear" Footing

Five years on the UNOS list waiting for a donation for a liver transplant was making me crazy. In need of a change, I convinced my husband to move to the Midwest for an opportunity to help a startup technology company go to market.

Shortly after moving, I was referred to a top transplant doctor who located a "perfect match" organ six months later. I had refused to think about the 30% success rate predicted for my liver transplant.

Eighteen hours after being wheeled into the operating room I woke briefly, smiled at my husband, and went back to sleep for another eight hours. But what I knew was, I had made it. I'd beat the odds. It was a huge pivotal moment.

Back at work six weeks later, I was testing a new marketing and website software platform, and we were preparing to onboard our fourth customer. As the only non-techie in the startup company—and with marketing and business operations experience—it fell to me to provide the training and help the customer's marketing team implement the platform.

Back then, company websites were an act of moving print brochures into digital format. The resulting websites were bland and boring with no thought about the target audience they needed to attract.

It bothered me. Especially when we started hearing things like:

- There's no impact
- Nothing's changed for us
- Where are the sales inquiries?

As an avid fiction writer (who had attended writing retreats led by best-selling authors and whose unpublished manuscript had been a finalist in a nationwide novel contest) it occurred to me that I could help our customers improve their content and how they presented it digitally.

When I met with them to help them use our software platform more effectively, I saw characters and heard stories that had meaning. Now, I needed to help them get that feeling into their content.

I spent time learning about their companies, products, customers, and buyers. And it dawned on me that if I could create a character (hero) strong enough to stand up to a 400-page plot with goals, conflict, mentors, antagonists, and challenges, that I could do the same with buyers navigating a complex purchasing process.

And it worked. It allowed me to help our customers use these buyer and customer insights to drive the "story" presented on their websites. Within a few years, I had so many requests for help from our customers that I didn't have time to do my job running the software company.

At the same time, my husband desperately wanted to move back to our home in Palm Desert, California. I was terrified. I'd finally found work I loved and was being pulled to move away from it.

That's when my husband suggested I start my consulting business. Content marketing was in its early stages. Remote work was becoming acceptable. But the fear was palpable. What if it didn't work? What if I couldn't do it?

Then I got a call from an agent who asked if I wanted to turn the blog I'd started writing into a book. And when I floated the consulting idea to a few of our customers, they asked how they could sign up to continue working with me.

So I leaped into my next huge pivotal moment. After all, I'd already beaten the biggest odds I'd likely ever confront seven years earlier.

Eighteen years later, I'm still having the most fun ever! Getting to turn a hobby I love into a well-paying career is a pivotal moment I'll always be grateful I acted on.

ARDATH ALBEE is a B2B Marketing Strategist and CEO of Marketing Interactions. She's an author, storyteller, and buyer-obsessed content wonk who helps companies connect with buyers and customers.

Chapter 18
Gaining New Perspectives

Sometimes we feel stuck. We aspire to a future that isn't quite working out. We think that our options are limited and don't know what to do. But even these challenging situations can be opportunities in disguise.

Dao's Defining Moment

Most kids have a limited view of what they want to be when they grow up. A firefighter, a doctor, or a teacher. They don't know all that's possible.

I felt the same way growing up in the USA as an immigrant refugee from Vietnam. I believed in the American dream—that ANYTHING was possible. I loved politics. And I even believed I could be the first Asian president of the United States.

Why did I think I could have a chance at that? (Besides the fact that I didn't qualify since I wasn't born here). At seventeen, I attended my state's YMCA Youth in Government program. The 1,000 students attending voted me as their youth governor. I was the first Asian elected to that top position.

***

Following along those lines, in my thirties, I couldn't accept that there was a glass ceiling for women in the corporate world. As an ambitious, impatient mother of four, I never took off more than the six weeks for maternity leave. I wanted to jump back on the corporate ladder as fast as I could.

However, after not being selected for the role of chief of staff to the CEO of Symantec—even though I was one of the top performers in the company—I knew it was time to leave.

I decided to get a job in an organization where I could be a bigger fish in a smaller pond. Yet even in those growing tech companies, I ran into career friction.

Fortunately, I had an honest, caring manager, Rich Baumgart, who saw people's potential and believed in giving women a chance.

He told me that my aspiration to become a senior executive at a Fortune 500 company wasn't likely to happen. And he said that my time at the company wasn't going to last long.

Apparently, all my ideas for improving things and my style of selling were driving the CEO nuts.

Then he told me, "Dao, you have what it takes to go into business by yourself." Having worked with me for over a year, he saw in me a capable entrepreneur. Someone who was bright, thought outside the box, and didn't take no for an answer very easily. I'd never even thought that starting a business could be a career option.

THAT was the defining moment in my life. A trajectory that I could have never imagined at thirty-five years old.

I didn't know how to start a business or what the company would be selling but I knew that doing the same things I'd been doing for the past decade wasn't going to get me where I wanted to be.

So, at the age of thirty-seven I bootstrapped an Amazon cloud computing company. A few years later, I received a scholarship to a three-year Harvard business CEO executive program to become a more educated entrepreneur.

We quickly became one of the fifty fastest-growing women-owned companies in the US. Not long after, I sold my company to a large Brazilian corporation.

Life is like the game of Chutes and Ladders. It's never a straight ladder to your dreams but if you're resilient and willing to take another ladder you'll find your way to your greatest fulfilling aspiration!

DAO JENSEN, refugee-turned-entrepreneur, built a company driven by purpose—proving that vision and grit can create a life beyond expectations. Even when your aspiration shatters, you can find a purpose that matters!

The Question that Lit a Spark

It had been a tough few years. With a colleague, I'd launched a company that provided online assessment tools to help organizations with their hiring process. Almost immediately, we landed some marquee clients. The future looked bright.

Then the 2008 recession hit—and we had no business. Zippo. All that work for nothing but debt. It took a while for me to get my feet on the ground again. I scrambled to bring in money by doing consulting work.

Finally, a new opportunity popped up. An acquaintance who was starting a new company asked me if I'd come on board to help launch their chemical-free cleaning product. The results looked impressive, so I said yes.

But in less than a year, a large potential client informed me that their lab tests weren't achieving the same results that the company touted. I was stunned. Then I learned senior management had falsified the product's effectiveness with the Environmental Protection Agency. The investors shut the company down virtually overnight.

I was out of work again. This time, I was on unemployment for a few months and had to participate in the Dislocated Worker Program. Not only did it take up a lot of time, but it was a dehumanizing experience. After decades of doing well, I felt humiliated and demoralized.

I had to find a job fast, as I was functionally broke, having been relieved of my financial assets in a recent divorce. Fortunately, a friend introduced me to a young entrepreneur who had a software idea for businesses. I was intrigued. After a few follow-up meetings, I joined his small team.

But I found myself at a professional crossroads. I felt stuck, limited by my lack of technical credentials, which could have opened new doors. Over breakfast with my nineteen-year-old daughter Hayden, I shared my lingering regret about never finishing my engineering degree.

She said, "Why don't you go back to school and get your engineering degree?"

That question sparked a shift. It had never dawned on me. I began exploring programs offered through the local university's engineering department. That fall, I enrolled in the Master of Science in Management of Technology (MOT) program, which was essentially an "MBA for techies."

It was the perfect bridge between my business experience and the technical foundation I needed to move forward with confidence. Plus, it energized me again. I was with a younger group of people. They were curious, engaging, and challenging.

During my classes, I found myself taking a double set of notes. The first set was focused on what I needed for the class. But the second set of notes was more important to me. It contained thoughts about what I could have done differently in the past two tech companies I'd previously started.

It also gave me ideas about App Data Room, another software product that this young company had developed. It allowed marketers to distribute digital product information to their sales teams. While it only had a few customers, I saw its untapped potential.

I presented the owners with a business plan built around this product. In July 2013, we launched App Data Room LLC and bootstrapped its growth to $3 million in under three years. At that point, we were acquired by venture capital and changed our name to Modus.

When we reached $5 million, the investors wanted to hire a younger CEO. I supported this decision because it was best for the company, employees, and their families.

But the reality is, none of this would have happened if my daughter hadn't asked me that one question.

ORRIN BROBERG is a trusted advisor to leadership teams. He helps businesses scale by strategically engaging customers, employees, and channel partners. As a successful entrepreneur, he fosters alignment and drives sustainable growth.

I Was Determined

I had always dreamt of going to college. Instead, I married early, became a mother at eighteen, divorced at twenty-six, and was the primary caregiver for my two kids. Despite working full-time and doing side jobs to scrape by, I lived at the poverty line. With minimal child support, there were months when my paycheck couldn't cover rent and daycare.

I needed a change, and I felt that a college degree was the only way to get there. But how could I make it happen?

At the time, I worked at Coors. After starting as a beer trailer clerk, I was now a secretary. One day, I met Pearl, a temp and a part-time college student. When I told her about my dream and how impossible it felt, she replied, "Why don't you take just one class? That's one less class to take later."

A lightbulb switched on—no, more like a spotlight. Before long, I discovered that Coors had an 80% tuition reimbursement program. I enrolled in one night class … then another … and another. My kids often came with me and played in the hall. After they went to bed, I studied. I was exhausted, running on caffeine and determination, but I was on a mission.

Seven years later, I received my bachelor's degree. I felt an overwhelming sense of pride and accomplishment that I'd never known before!

Now, I needed to put that marketing degree to work! But I had to find a way to launch my new career without leaving my full-time job. So, I wrote a letter pitching a marketing internship on my own time. I emphasized how much Coors had already invested in me and then wrote, "Want to see a great ROI on your tuition investment?"

I sent it to every marketing director and vice president at Coors. I called their assistants to get on their bosses' calendars. It was intimidating, but I was driven. Nothing was going to stop me.

After several weeks, I got an email from a Coors HR director asking me to come to her office. When I sat down nervously, she asked me, "How would you feel about sales?" It caught me completely off guard.

It turns out I'd been so persistent that upper management told her, "Do something with her, she's driving us all crazy!" The HR director must have sensed the potential in my intense ambition and dogged persistence.

When I agreed, she placed me in a year-long training program and offered me a full-time sales position. As a trainee, I attended sampling events in bars and on college campuses, but as a mom of two preteens, promoting alcoholic beverages to young people was incongruent with who I was.

Instead, I wanted to sell a product that helped people. So, after a year on the road, I began interviewing with pharmaceutical and medical device companies. After many interviews, a small startup medical device company took a chance on me as an entry-level salesperson.

Driven to validate my hard work and long path, I quickly became their top performer. Soon, their much larger competitor recruited me at a significantly higher salary. Before long, that led to my promotion to territory manager, overseeing four states. Over a twenty-year career, I consistently hit or exceeded my goals, even achieving number one multiple times.

Some thirty years after earning my degree, I often reflect on this arduous journey. Whenever the goal or objective seems too large to overcome, I remember Pearl's advice to "just take one class."

I take a step, then another, then another, until I conquer the monster that once stood in front of me.

LORI CHESTER was an award-winning sales manager in medical devices. She's currently a certified veterinary technician and studying plant-based nutrition. She lives in Colorado with her husband, two dogs, and four donkeys.

Rule One Magic

I've experienced so many pivotal moments, one might think my left foot lives on a lazy Susan. But perhaps the biggest turnabout came at the hands of a quiet man who used to visit my mother's antique store.

Her dusty shop held a riot of beauties in search of beholders, from shabby Hoosier cabinets and glossy Duncan Phyfe dining sets to dainty Victorian ephemera; pearl-handled, gold-tipped pens; and useless but funky old cameras.

Gerry ignored all that. He came to play the piano.

A surly oak upright monstrosity that nobody wanted, the piano came with the shop. After a brief trip to our house, where I failed to master it, it sulked under the stairs leading down to the basement shop. It represented my musical failures; that is, until Gerry found it, tuned it, and brought his friend Fred to play honky-tonk-tinged, four-handed sonatas and joyous, improvised stride-style jazz.

They'd slip in quietly. Even the music of the little bell on the door failed to announce their presence. Not a word was spoken. They played softly, gaining momentum, and finally chortling with laughter. Glued to my stool behind the register, too shy to get closer, I'd peek up from my book to watch at a distance.

Practiced old friends, their bodies danced on the bench as they made room for each other at the keyboard, one's hand up and over, the other's gliding deftly up the keyboard. They'd play until the sunlight turned floating dust motes into golden embers, buy something unnecessary and small, paying for the privilege to play without risking insulting us with much-needed charity, and slip out the door, ringing its bell on the way out.

One day, while Gerry paid for one of the railroad postcards he pretended to collect, he paused to study a photograph my mother's partner had taped up near the register. "What an evocative photo. May I look more closely?" After studying it, he asked who took it. I explained it was just a snapshot of the partner's daughter I'd taken because she looked so sad yet beautiful sitting in the tall grass behind our house that day.

"Mind how you talk about your work. It's never 'just,' you know? This is well-seen, well-captured. And well—what camera did you use?" I confessed, I'd stolen my mother's Instamatic. He chuckled, gently put the photo back, and went home.

The next time, Gerry came alone. He didn't play the piano but came straight to the register and pushed a red box labeled Alpa at me. Inside was the most beautiful vintage camera I had ever beheld. Not new, but flawlessly maintained.

I thought he wanted to sell it and began to redirect him to someone I knew would give him the best value. We couldn't afford it. He guffawed so loudly that I jumped. "No! No, no!" he snorted. "This is for you!"

And while I stood there making stunned fish faces, he continued, "There are two conditions. Rule One: You may not thank me. Ever. Do something for someone else, and that's enough. Rule Two: I have signed you up for two courses in photography and darkroom techniques. I'll know if you don't show up. Oh, yes, and Fred will bring the darkroom gear you will need to your house. Do the work. Got it?"

I started to blither thanks, and he interrupted. "Breaking Rule One so soon?" I shut up and examined this extraordinary treasure.

The light changed. I looked up. Gerry vanished like one of those golden embers that surrounded him when he played the piano. I never saw him again.

His camera changed my life, became my voice, and an integral part of my later work with media technologies, graphics programming, and art.

But what made that a pivotal moment on the lazy Susan of my life? On that day, I learned that what we need will find us, and by Gerry's example, we can honor these gifts by providing pivotal opportunities for others with the courage to say yes.

Gerry's gift put me on a path, with all its twists and turns, that led me to a place where I am putting cameras, computers, and training in the hands of young adults whose circumstances aren't equal to their many gifts as human beings.

And I'm not going to break the Rule One magic by saying thank you. And I don't let them say it, either.

DAWN STOCKBRIDGE EPSTEIN, creative strategist and founder of animation studio Blue Cormorant, turns questions into stories that inform, spark empathy, and inspire lasting change.

Up the Hill

"Okay, we have .7 miles until we get on I-80." My mom and I were driving to Mankato to visit a small two-year business school where I had already mapped out my future: attend for two years, earn a medical secretarial degree, marry my high school boyfriend, and live happily ever after.

After meeting with the admissions team, Mom casually said, "Well, I've heard there's another school in town—Mankato State University. Should we take a look?"

"Sure, why not."

I pulled out the map, and we made our way across town and up the hill. As we pulled onto the campus, I was struck by the scene: multiple buildings, sprawling lawns, and students bustling between classes. I remember thinking, "Wow, this looks like something straight out of the movies." After a few wrong turns and kind directions from strangers, we found the admissions office. They somehow squeezed us in even though we didn't have an appointment.

And there it was, a surprise—Mankato State offered a two-year medical secretarial program. I don't know why or how, but it was in their course catalog. I had a decision to make. Do I attend the one-story business school or a university teeming with energy? I chose the school "up the hill."

That decision changed my life. But it wasn't easy. On my first day of classes, I proudly wore my high school letter jacket, shiny track medals and all. The looks I got ranged from amused to pitiful, making it clear that I didn't fit in. I quietly retired the jacket that night feeling embarrassed and overwhelmed by my unfamiliar environment. What had I done?

My first course in chemistry didn't help. I kept looking left and right to see if the other students were understanding what the professor was teaching. It sounded like Greek to me and self-doubt and self-talk set in. "You don't have what it takes. You should have enrolled at the business school."

However, that negative self-talk changed when I took a class in Community Health 101. There I met Professor Bruno Willinski. He was unlike anyone I'd ever met. His passion for teaching was contagious—so contagious that when he got excited, his face would turn bright red, and occasionally, a little "spray" would accompany his enthusiasm.

Watching him, I thought, "I want to do what he's doing. I want to teach." It was another turn in the road.

I changed my major from a two-year degree to a four-year degree in Community Health Education. Earning a four-year degree had never been part of my original plan. In high school, I got good grades. However, I was more interested in being president of the pep club and captain of the dance team. But I buckled down, spent countless hours in the library, and became the first in my family to graduate from college.

I didn't marry my high school boyfriend. I did, however, end up being a teacher in a variety of roles. Right out of college, I worked for the American Cancer Society teaching cancer education classes. During the fitness craze of the 1980s, I taught Jazzercise and became a member of their first training team. And today, I teach emotional intelligence and sales leadership workshops.

In each role, I've tried to remember that eighteen-year-old girl who felt lost and out of place by encouraging others, "You've got what it takes."

I've channeled my inner Bruno Willinski, bringing enthusiasm to each teaching opportunity. And yes, I warn my students that when I get excited, they might experience a little "spray" of passion too.

It's amazing how one unexpected turn up a hill—and one passionate teacher—can change the entire course of a life.

COLLEEN STANLEY is the author of four books focused on mentorship, emotional intelligence, and sales. She helps individuals and companies bridge "knowing and doing" gaps in life and business.

Breaking Out of Poverty Required Heartbreaking Decisions

"How can you help your mom if you only earn $8 an hour?" My college professor asked me this brutally direct question.

It was a few days before my junior year. I'd called her in tears, asking if I should drop out, risking my seat in the class and scholarships.

Why? Just a few weeks earlier, I'd admitted my mom to the hospital to treat Stage IV cancer. The doctors said she could be there for months.

It was just the two of us. Money was tight. Now, because Mom couldn't work, we couldn't afford our rental home, so I moved in with my aunt.

That's when I asked my professor the question that had consumed my summer…

"Do I drop out and work at the local recreation center? Or do I finish my degree for a shot at a high-paying career?"

She bluntly told me that a minimum-wage job wasn't a path out of my family's challenges. It wouldn't cover our bills or offer a path to full-time work. Plus, with only a high school diploma, I'd be hard-pressed to find better options. Besides, my mom was in the hospital, so I wouldn't be any help as a caretaker.

She was right, but I didn't feel any better. But my mom was furious that I'd even considered it. She encouraged (or rather, demanded) that I stay in school.

After making that hard decision, I knew I couldn't waste the opportunity. I would graduate with a job that would give us both a comfortable life.

Motivated by dwindling cash and ever-lingering guilt, I saw each day as a chance to support my family. I studied harder to get straight A's, found part-time jobs, and networked with successful alumni weekly.

My mom finally left the medical facility a year later to stay in low-income housing. Around that time, I landed two job offers each with enough income to cover our bills and replenish our savings.

But which one should I take? Both were management consulting roles that could serve as a launch pad for a successful career.

- Option 1 was in Washington, D.C. helping the government expand social service programs and spend tax dollars more efficiently.
- Option 2 was in Los Angeles, helping Fortune 500 companies optimize stock options in executive compensation packages. It paid 25% more.

I called my mom for her opinion. She told me she was proud of me for making the tough decision to stay in school and for landing these offers. Then, she reminded me that making money was never my goal. My goal had always been to help my community.

She gave me her blessing to take the Washington job. I signed the offer that night.

***

Working in public service satisfied my deep desire to give back, especially when I supported programs helping low-income kids.

With financial security, I redirected my time to building my career. My work advising federal agencies led to collaborations with the White House and billion-dollar foundations to reduce poverty and promote equality.

I applied to grad school and secured a scholarship for a dual degree from Wharton and Harvard. Plus, my volunteer work with international nonprofits turned into meaningful board positions.

Reflecting on those early critical decisions, I realize how they laid the foundations for my principles. Staying in school forced me to acknowledge my limitations, think long-term, and push myself to make the most of the opportunities I was given.

Choosing the public service role revealed that following my values leads to more success than following the money.

Together, they created a framework for a life of purpose that is bigger and fuller than my mom or I would have ever thought possible.

MICHAEL NELSON is a social innovation expert. He helps governments, nonprofits, and changemakers better serve their communities with leading technology and program design.

Chapter 19
Embracing Opportunities

Occasionally, we're in the right place at the right time. Yet all too often, when that happens, fear rears its ugly head or we miss seeing the potential. But in truth, it's beckoning us in a new life-giving direction.

Pivoting Into the Startup World

In the past forty-five years, I've helped scale six startup companies, including two unicorns. I was the first salesperson and the sixth employee at HubSpot, an innovative software company that scaled to $2.4 billion during my seventeen-year tenure.

But the pivotal moment in my entire career was my first startup.

In 1981, I worked as a salesperson for a mid-sized computer store in downtown Boston. I sold Apple computers to corporate accounts. Roger, my boss, was a friendly former band leader from Wisconsin.

He was a good people manager and a real straight shooter. He followed the rules, didn't swear, and wore a tie every day. He shielded us from the corporate noise and tried to maintain a light culture. We almost always hit quota.

One day, Roger came into the store and announced that he was quitting to work at a startup.

"What's a startup?" I asked innocently.

"It's a small company that grows quickly," he said.

Happy for him, I wished him good luck!

"I want to take you with me!" he announced.

I said, "But I already have a job."

He replied, "I'll give you $75.00 more in salary per month!"

"OK, I am IN!" I said. That was a lot of money in those days.

In 1982, I left with Roger and went to work for Businessland, a San Jose-based computer hardware and software startup. They were a computer reseller that sold Apple and IBM computers, networks, software, and training to companies.

In just nine years, the company scaled from $100,000 to $1.4 billion. I started as a salesperson and filled several management roles throughout my tenure.

If Roger hadn't asked me to join, I would never have had the opportunity of being a sales leader at one of the world's fastest-growing companies. Nor would I have met Bill Gates, Steve Jobs, Ray Norda, Dave Norman, and other key tech executives of the era.

But the story gets even better…

Two days after I started working at Businessland, I was summoned to attend a meeting at a prestigious law firm on State Street in Boston. It turns out that, unbeknownst to me as a twenty-two-year-old, I'd signed a noncompete agreement when I started with my old company. As a result, I was prohibited from working for a competitor within 250 miles (noncompetes were enforceable in those days).

Several calls were exchanged between the legal teams of both companies. I sat and listened to a bunch of high-priced lawyers yelling at each other. It was both interesting and scary.

After hours of negotiation, Dave, the CEO of Businessland, called Roger and me on a separate line and said, "Your old company will release you from your noncompete if we pay them $250,000." That's a lot of money today but was even more in 1982.

He then asked Roger, "Is this guy worth that kind of money?" WHILE I WAS LISTENING TO THE CALL. I'm not sure the CEO remembered that I was on the line because he wasn't a mean guy.

Roger said, "He's absolutely worth it!"

Boom. So I got hired by Businessland and spent nine years grinding out eighty-hour weeks, earning my entrepreneurial chops. #ohbaby

If those two pivotal moments hadn't fallen my way, I would have had a completely different career trajectory—amazing, incredible, and exciting. I'll always be thankful to Roger Lund and Dave Norman (and hundreds of others) for the opportunity.

Even better, for thirty-five years, I've been married to the beautiful, smart, wisdom-filled Amy Tyre. We've raised two socially responsible children.

DAN TYRE, CEO of Tyre Angel, advises dozens of companies on growing in today's global economy. He's also a speaker, author, executive coach, investor, board member, and more.

My Worst Christmas Gift Became My Greatest Fortune

I still remember the crushing disappointment I felt that Christmas morning in Chicago. As a young Korean immigrant child, I had one wish that year—the original Nintendo that all my American friends were getting.

***

Money was tight for my family; my parents were struggling to learn English while finding jobs to support us. We rarely had new things, we mostly made do with hand-me-downs.

When I spotted that promising rectangular box under the tree, wrapped in festive paper, my heart raced. This was it—my parents had somehow found a way to get me a Nintendo!

I tore through the wrapping paper with the unbridled excitement only a child can muster. But instead of the gaming console I'd dreamed of, I found myself staring at a Radio Shack TRS-80 computer.

***

My father stood behind me, his expression a mixture of pride and determination. "This is a computer and it's the future," he said firmly. "You need to learn this."

I was devastated. I didn't want the future—I wanted what my friends had now. I cried harder than I had about anything before.

Through my tears, I couldn't possibly understand the sacrifice my parents had made. That TRS-80—a precursor to the Tandy 1000 and one of the first personal computers—represented a significant portion of my family's modest income.

***

But my father's decision was final. I had to learn to use this strange machine with its blinking cursor and command prompts.

No Super Mario Bros. for me—instead, I was typing rudimentary programming commands and learning how computers worked from the inside out.

Years passed, and that Christmas disappointment faded into memory. But the skills I developed from that unwanted gift? They grew.

In college, I gravitated naturally toward computer science, building on the foundation that had been forced upon me years earlier.

I continued exploring computational techniques, including early technologies that would eventually lead to today's generative AI systems.

***

Now, as an AI expert making a significant impact in my field, I can trace my entire professional trajectory back to that Christmas morning when I didn't get a Nintendo.

What seemed like the worst gift possible turned out to be the greatest fortune of my life.

***

I understand now what my father knew then—he wasn't just buying me a computer; he was investing in my future at great personal sacrifice.

That pivotal moment, born from childish tears and parental wisdom, shaped everything that followed.

Sometimes our greatest disappointments truly are blessings in disguise, wrapped in unexpected packages under the Christmas tree.

JOE YUN is CEO of bluefoxlabs.ai and leads AI initiatives at the University of Pittsburgh. He helps individuals and businesses future-proof themselves for an AI-driven world.

The First Step Forward

At sixty, I stand at the helm of my consulting firm, a thriving global enterprise dedicated to helping organizations and people identify their purpose and maximize their excellence.

I work in nearly every sector—energy, media, travel, automotive, manufacturing, healthcare, technology, education, construction, finance, and government. Over the years, I've assessed, advised, coached, and mentored hundreds of companies and thousands of leaders and students.

But the moment that changed everything happened three decades earlier, when I was twenty-nine. That's when I was offered my first formal leadership role.

I still remember the fluorescent lights of that narrow conference room where my manager had tapped me for a team lead position. It was a sudden promotion. My predecessor had resigned without notice. The team was demoralized. Deadlines loomed. Tensions ran high.

I accepted the role, heart pounding. I didn't feel ready, but something inside me—a quiet conviction rooted in my core values—told me this was my time to step forward.

The first challenge wasn't the project. It was the behavior of my coworkers.

The team I inherited had splintered into cliques where distrust ran rampant and several felt overlooked for the position I now held. "You're too young," one colleague muttered. Another simply refused to engage.

I could have leaned into positional authority, but I didn't. Instead, I led with vulnerability and what I valued most: trust, respect, fairness, and integrity.

I started by listening. In one-on-one meetings, open forums, and anonymous surveys, I asked, "What do you need to do your best work?" and "What would make this team whole again?"

Then I acted. I removed legacy barriers, reallocated workloads fairly, and consistently recognized team wins. I owned my mistakes publicly and gave credit freely.

I didn't try to have all the answers. Instead, I created "space for grace," a space for the team to productively dialogue, debate, and co-create innovative and effective solutions.

It was exhausting and energizing all at once. There were nights I cried, in fear and joy, in my car on the drive home. To my surprise, it was working.

I also began a practice that's stayed with me: daily reflection. I would ask myself three questions, journal my answers every night, and reflect weekly on where I was:

1. Did I lead with integrity?
2. Did I elevate others?
3. Did I align with my motivators and strengths?

My top strengths—strategic thinking, compassion, and activating potential—fueled my leadership philosophy. I discovered my greatest motivator wasn't recognition or reward—it was helping others find meaning and activating motivation to be effective and thrive. That became my compass, shaping every role I held thereafter.

That first leadership role became my crucible. The project exceeded its goals, and the team stayed intact. More importantly, people started to believe again—in themselves, in each other, in their work, and in me as their leader.

Years later, I would reflect on that season as the moment my purpose crystallized: to create work environments where people feel seen, heard, valued, and empowered to give their best. It was the same ethos I carried into executive leadership when co-founding my firm to shape the next generation of leaders.

I consult, coach, and advise my clients that performance thrives on deep self-awareness, self-mastery, and psychological safety; that culture is built in the spaces between people; and that excellence isn't an output—it's a way of being and becoming.

As I close my journal every evening, I smile. "The hardest thing about that first leadership role," I often tell clients and mentees, "was not the decisions I had to make. It was learning to lead without losing myself."

I never did and still am. And for that, I am forever grateful.

LORI HARRIS is Partner and Principal Consultant at Harris Whitesell Consulting, a Certified Executive Coach, and host of the Maximize Excellence! podcast, driving organizational and leadership excellence and transformation.

When a War Changes Your Map

I didn't plan to move across the world. I didn't even plan to leave my city. But in 2022, like many Ukrainians, I found myself living in a version of reality that no one could've predicted.

At the time, I was in Kharkiv, just twenty miles from the Russian border. Sirens, fear, and uncertainty had become part of everyday life—but that was only the surface. There were explosions, the roar of military planes overhead, flashes in the sky at night, and the terrible sound of something crashing in the distance. There were deaths. Real ones. People we knew, or people just like us. I remember the fear of even leaving the basement—the feeling that stepping outside could mean not coming back.

And yet, in the middle of all this, I decided to sign up for online English conversation lessons. I thought, "If I'm stuck here, I might as well keep learning something." I didn't know it yet, but that one small decision would change everything.

The program matched Ukrainians with English speakers around the world. And somehow, I got paired with a woman living in Minneapolis. Out of all the people in the world—it was her.

I truly believe the universe sent her into my life exactly when I needed someone.

We started talking in May. At first, it was just about language and culture, but slowly, we began to talk about life, our dreams, and our fears. A month later, she said something that made my heart stop, "What if you came to the US?"

I didn't know how to respond. Who offers something like that after just a few weeks of calls? But at the same time, something in me lit up—a tiny spark that whispered, "What if this is the beginning of something new?

In August 2022, I made my decision. It wasn't easy. At that time, my mom and grandma were living in an occupied area, and we were separated. I didn't know when I'd see them again—or if I even would. The idea of being even farther from them was painful. But I needed their opinion. I asked them what they thought about the move—and despite everything, they supported me completely.

The months that followed were filled with paperwork, nerves, and questions. There were rumors going around that even if your US travel authorization was approved, it could suddenly be canceled—even mid-flight. We didn't know if we'd be let in or turned away at the border. We were flying on pure faith.

But on January 24, 2023, we arrived in America.

Starting over wasn't easy. Everything was new—the language, the culture, the rhythm of daily life.

In Ukraine, I never used English outside of lessons. Here, it was everywhere—in grocery stores, pharmacies, neighbors, and appointments. I was initially scared to speak. What if I said something wrong? But every conversation became a little victory.

And then there were things that shocked me in unexpected ways.

I remember walking outside at night and seeing the streets brightly lit—it felt almost unreal. Back home, the lights stayed off at night because of air raids and safety concerns. And here, people were walking, laughing, and carefree.

I kept thinking that they don't even realize how lucky they are. They don't know what it means to wait in silence for the power to come back. They don't know what it's like to flinch at every loud sound."

And most of all, they don't realize how small most problems are once you've seen what real fear, loss, and survival feel like.

Soon came new routines, new connections, and little by little—a sense of home. I'll always miss Ukraine. But this chapter gave me not just safety, but something else I hadn't expected—the freedom to rebuild, to dream, and to grow.

That pivotal moment—saying yes to someone who believed in me, even from across the world, and feeling supported by my family—changed the course of my life. I didn't know exactly where it would lead. But deep down, I knew it was the right step.

YULIIA YURCHUK is a Ukrainian-born marketing specialist rebuilding her career in the US after relocating from Ukraine, helping businesses grow online with creative content, social media, and digital strategy.

The Award That Changed Everything

I'm staring at an email inviting me to submit my presentation for the Annual Prezi Awards. It's mid-December 2013, and I'm at a crossroads. Six months earlier, I had quit my full-time job to become a consultant in my previous field of electronic security. It had been a bold move, and it wasn't paying off.

After six months of limited traction, I'm facing a harsh reality. In January, I'll need to start applying for jobs again. My entrepreneurial experiment gasps on life support.

Prezi, an alternative to PowerPoint, has become my preferred presentation tool. I leveraged it extensively in my previous role. I believe wholeheartedly in its dynamic, nonlinear approach and excellent functionality on tablets. It was a game-changer for in-person meetings.

The irony of the moment isn't lost on me. The presentation I'm considering submitting is the very one I've been using to pitch my consulting services during those struggling six months. I'd also used it on some well-received industry webinars. Yet I haven't been able to close the prospective clients I had hoped for.

Having used Prezi for years, I've seen countless incredible designs from talented creative professionals. I'm confident my work doesn't measure up. Imposter syndrome hits hard. Who's even working right now anyway? It's almost the holidays.

My finger hovers over the Submit button. I am this close to not entering at all.

Despite my doubts, I decided to give it a shot and offer my presentation, "Tablets for Security Consultants: 5 Ways to Maximize ROI."

On December 28, while most people were still in holiday mode, the email that changed everything arrived.

I had won the "Best Business Prezi of 2013" award! The recognition came right at the deadline of my self-imposed ultimatum to return to the corporate world.

The impact was immediate and transformative. I was featured in a press release that ran in the Chicago Tribune. I began offering my services on freelancing sites, highlighting the award prominently, and started winning paid jobs!

My pivot away from electronic security opened up a whole new world of potential clients who needed help from the "Best Business Prezi" award winner. The next six months told an entirely different financial story than the previous ones, generating enough business momentum that I never had to submit those job applications.

The award didn't just validate my work—it completely reshaped my vision and triggered a career transformation. In 2014, I became a certified Prezi Expert featured prominently on their website. New clients called and opportunities multiplied.

I built a full-fledged presentation agency, Puffingston Presentations, which grew to a team of ten, working with world-renowned clients such as Dell, IBM, Siemens, and Western Union. We crafted presentations for C-suite executives and speakers at prominent business events, including CES, TEDx, and SXSW.

As part of my Prezi Expert status, I was flown to Budapest multiple times to meet with experts from around the world. I also met with Prezi's C-suite executives at their corporate headquarters. In just one year, I had gone from retreating to the safety of a traditional job to connecting with creative minds globally.

After a decade running this creative agency, I leveraged all I'd learned to pivot again—this time becoming a global keynote speaker on employee engagement, digital natives, AI, and the Future of

Work. Today, I still apply many of the presentation principles that helped me win that award so many years ago.

All of this—my entire career trajectory—hung from the thinnest thread of courage, that moment when I almost didn't click Submit but found the will to try anyway.

LUKE GOETTING is a Future of Work expert and global keynote speaker who has captivated audiences at TEDx, DisruptHR, the Global Project Management Forum, and hundreds of other events worldwide.

It Started on a Ski Lift

I was at Heavenly Valley Ski Resort at Lake Tahoe, riding up the chairlift. The guy sitting next to me introduced himself and then said, "Tell me about yourself…"

I responded, "I'm about to enter the PhD program for Applied Physics at UC Berkeley. When I get my PhD, I plan to be a professor and researcher."

He said, "That's really cool! I'm an artist, designer, and sometime inventor."

After a few minutes, he asked, "Do you mind if I bounce an idea off you?" He went on to describe something he was prototyping and some of the problems he was having with it.

I asked a few questions, but by that time we had to get off the chairlift. We agreed to meet at the bottom of the mountain and ride back up together.

We spent the afternoon riding the lift up the mountain, talking about ideas and things he might try. We would ski down, then meet up again and ride the lift, sharing more ideas.

***

At the end of the day, I said, "Give me your contact information. Let me think about this, I'll send you some stuff."

On the drive back down to Berkeley, I thought about the ideas and a research/test plan. At home I wrote it up and sent it to him.

A few days later he called, we talked about the ideas for a while, then he said, "Would you be interested in joining my company as Vice President of Engineering and Product Design?"

Here it was, almost a classic Silicon Valley story. I thought, "I'm twenty-one years old. I've never held a real job, and this guy is asking me to be a vice president! And it's really a cool product! What if we could make it work?"

My sponsor at Berkeley tried to talk me out of it. He thought I should pursue my studies, research, and teach.

It didn't take me long. I accepted the job.

***

It was enormous fun. People started getting interested; some were looking to invest. We were facing some monstrous challenges. We could make the prototypes work, but there were always some problems with them. We struggled to overcome the problems.

About eighteen months later, we failed. We shut our doors. Even though it didn't work out, it was probably one of the best learning experiences I've had.

I realized that business success is about much more than a cool product. I also learned that perhaps our own egos were limiting us. We had people interested in licensing our technology, but we thought, "Why should we give it up now? We can do much more ourselves." We discovered too late that we really needed those resources to help us move forward.

All these lessons were foundational to my next moves in business and the lessons have stayed with me ever since.

Ironically, about twelve years after we shut down, Honda introduced a technology very similar to that we had been developing. They had overcome the challenges we faced and taken it far beyond our imaginations. Today, that technology sits in about every Honda vehicle and others are licensing it as well. Another lesson learned.

DAVE BROCK, CEO at Partners in EXCELLENCE and author of *Sales Manager Survival Guide*, practices ruthless pragmatism to mask his unwavering idealism. He's committed to obsessive learning and relentless execution.

Chapter 20
Getting Unstuck

Changing how we think can be challenging. We're following long-held expectations for us. Or, with the way things are going, we can't see a future for ourselves. It's only by shifting our thinking that we can find our strengths.

The Ultimate Pivot

You don't have to see a way for there to be a way.

At the age of twenty-two, a young man stood in the kitchen of a house where he was living alone in the woods. The point of a large butcher knife rested against his stomach in preparation for what was next. Both of his hands gripped the handle, ready to plunge it in.

He felt his life had already ended, so this was the only thing left for him to do, to make an exit before all the looming harms could complete their work.

He paused to review all the problems pressing on him, all the terrible developments that had torn away the future for which he'd hoped. They seemed so overwhelming, so utterly impossible to solve.

But with that judgement, a spark of something began to form, the merest hint of an inner attitude he had not experienced in all this. It soon ignited a tiny flame of curiosity that quickly grew into an intense wonder at the magnitude of what we human beings in the world can face.

And this instantly led to an intense interest and then a need to see how it would all turn out, the sum of all the awfulness. He was suddenly more intrigued than in despair. It was all too fascinating.

Then in the next instant he realized he had to stick around to witness what would happen next, and then after that, just to satisfy this powerful curiosity.

So, curiosity saved one cat. He put down the knife and took a deep breath. He resolved to live, to see it all through to whatever bitter end might ensue, just for the sake of knowing. He would face it and do his best to outlive it. And years later, he was immensely glad he did.

An otherwise normal, healthy young person freely living in the world contemplates suicide. Can it ever be rational for such a soul to take this path? I think not. The finality of the act is essentially incommensurate with the necessarily limited and incomplete perspective from which it's considered.

You don't have to see a way for there to be a way. That seems to be a teaching of all our great wisdom traditions. The world is richer with possibilities for the future than our inherently limited gaze can begin to grasp. Life is an ever-turning kaleidoscope of paths forward, endlessly churning up new options often beyond our ability to imagine.

The young man went on to study the wisdom traditions of the world, to earn two doctoral degrees from one of the world's top universities, to then teach at another one, to receive fellowships and awards for his work, and even to enjoy unexpected honorary doctorates for the difference he was perceived to have made in bringing wisdom to others.

As I write these words, it's been fifty-one wonderful years since that pivot. I know because of course I was the man who was yet to learn that you don't have to see a way for there to be a way.

A full marriage, great children, a wonderful grandchild, and many lovable pets, as well as over thirty books followed. So did an adventurous career after a second major pivot when I found the courage to leave the lifetime guarantee of a joyous job at a great institution to follow a new sense of calling: to go into the world where people live and bring them ideas they can use, and perhaps show them a new way ahead that they might for the first time be able to see.

TOM MORRIS is one of the most popular keynote speakers in the world. As a public philosopher and author of multiple bestselling books, he shares practical wisdom with great fun and good energy.

The Moment I Stopped Pretending

I was on a Zoom call presenting to the executive team, and I wanted to disappear.

The dog was barking. One kid was yelling, the other melting down over distance learning. My cat, in true dramatic form, was throwing up behind me. And I was presenting a high-stakes marketing strategy like everything was fine.

It wasn't.

We were a high-growth tech company, pushing forward when the world had hit pause in 2020. And I was doing what I always did—pushing too. I had built a successful career in marketing, climbing quickly, saying yes to everything.

I'd been a "fixer" since my teenage years. After losing my mom to cancer at thirteen, I became the girl who handled it all.

I was drawn to marketing not for the flashy campaigns, but for the psychology of helping people solve problems. And for better or worse, that made me a yes woman. Give me chaos, and I'll carry it.

Until I couldn't.

That day, in front of my team, trying to mute the noise while staying polished, something cracked. I wasn't just overwhelmed—I felt like I'd failed at everything.

I wanted to lock myself in a closet. I wanted out of my life. Behind the screen, no one said a word, but I had to pause. And right there, in that moment of pure unraveling, the tears came.

It was the moment I stopped pretending.

The truth was, I didn't recognize myself. I'd built a life to impress—chasing titles, praise, and validation. Success looked like more: more promotions, more projects, more people telling me I was crushing it.

I was balancing it all—corporate life, motherhood, and even helping my husband build an airplane while growing a YouTube channel. On paper, it was impressive. In reality, I was running on autopilot.

In the days that followed, I asked myself a hard question: What do I want?

And I didn't know. I'd spent so long pleasing everyone else that I had no idea what my own voice sounded like.

Leaving the corporate ladder was terrifying. I worried I was disappointing people. That I was quitting. But on January 1, 2022, I took on my employer as my first client and launched my own business.

Today, I live differently. I do work that lights me up with clients I admire, all on a schedule that protects my time and energy.

I help entrepreneurs grow businesses that are not just profitable, but purposeful—and that support their wellbeing.

I say no to things that don't fit, especially when it comes to my time. I've replaced perfection with alignment. And I'm still growing. Still curious. Still trying to serve with integrity and courage.

***

That pivotal moment on Zoom didn't break me. It brought me back to life.

COLLEEN KRANZ helps entrepreneurs grow a business—and life—that aligns. Through her Grow North Thursday newsletter and strategic advisory, she empowers founders to scale with purpose, profitability, and well-being.

I Thought I Wasn't Capable Until...

For almost forty years, I worked with self-employed professionals on how to attract clients. But the biggest challenge wasn't teaching marketing and sales techniques. It was helping clients overcome the fears, doubts, and hesitations that kept them from connecting with others.

Clients believed something bad would happen if they reached out—that they'd be rejected or embarrassed, or that they'd fail. Worse, they believed they had to get it all perfect before they started. These limiting beliefs fueled procrastination and anxiety.

For several years, I searched for an approach that would help my clients overcome their limiting beliefs. I found some useful things, but nothing transformational.

On the personal side, I was working with clients I liked. Overall, things were going well., Like any business owner, however, I experienced my share of ups and downs.

I was feeling stuck. For some unknown reason, I was procrastinating on everything. I had a long list of projects and couldn't seem to make any progress on them. I was feeling exactly like many of my stuck clients!

Then, in 2003, I discovered the book *Loving What Is* by Byron Katie. She taught a process for examining limiting beliefs and turning them into empowering beliefs. As soon as I started reading it, I knew I'd found what I'd been looking for to help my clients.

So, I dove into her process, called The Work, and began questioning my own limiting beliefs. What were the beliefs holding me back? And could I get beyond them?

The first step in The Work is to identify your limiting belief. The first time I did it, I wrote down several and eventually landed on this one:

"I'm just not capable."

Yes. That's exactly what I was feeling and what I believed.

The next step was to question it. "Is that belief true?" I paused … then burst out, "Who am I kidding? I'm the Action Plan Marketing Guy! I am capable. I know how to figure things out. I know how to get things done!" That belief was nonsense!

I sat there stunned. It was as if I'd awakened from a trance. What made me stuck only minutes before felt easy. My hesitation to move things forward turned into excitement to get moving.

I looked down at my project list, picked something, and took action. Then another. Then another. Over weeks and months, I filled notebooks with my limiting beliefs—undoing them one by one and accomplishing more than I had in years.

For months, I couldn't procrastinate if I tried. Things flowed. Projects got finished. Big successes followed. Whenever I got stuck, I sat down and did The Work process, discovered another limiting belief, and turned it around to an empowering belief. I felt unstoppable.

Soon after applying The Work to my life and business, I started sharing it with my clients and program participants. I'd finally found that hidden strategy that could help my clients get unstuck and move forward with less fear and resistance. Most of them experienced the same kind of breakthroughs I had.

Discovering The Work was the pivotal moment that transformed my life. I discovered that most of my limiting beliefs weren't true. And that life is much more about possibility, exploration, and discovery than we realize.

Now, twenty-two years later, I'm still exploring. Still experimenting. Still wondering what's next. When limiting beliefs are not an issue, life becomes a playground of possibilities.

And in this season of life—my so-called retirement—I'm even more excited about what's possible and the difference I can make.

ROBERT MIDDLETON, after working with self-employed professionals for forty years, now spends his retirement years writing articles about how to live a sane and joyous life.

Letting Go of My Father

Until I was seventeen, anyone looking at my life would've said I was lucky. I had a home, a family, and talent. Athletically, I stood out. I could disarm just about anyone with a mix of humor and intellect. I was also fortunate to have my older brother Jack—my best friend, protector, and a constant source of laughter. With Jack, I felt included and safe.

But what no one could see—including me—was the deep fear of loss and abandonment buried inside me. It was wrapped tight and tucked behind the jokes, the sports, and the smiles. I didn't even know it was there. But it was—always.

When I was seven, my father tried to take his own life. And then, just like that, he was gone. He disappeared—not just from the house, but from my world. He was institutionalized and remained away for seven years. When he finally came back, he was physically present but emotionally unavailable—a stranger in our home.

My mother held the family together. She was our rock. Strong, yes. But also impenetrable. Brilliant, stoic, and composed. She managed to keep us fed, clothed, and sheltered.

But her emotions were locked up. She never cried. Never cheered. Never scolded. Whether it was my father's breakdown, our own successes, or anything in between, her reaction was always the same: none.

Looking back, after years of therapy and meditation, I see now how early I learned the household rules: Don't feel too much. Don't need too much. And above all—don't show joy.

Somehow, my father's suffering had rewritten the emotional

code of the house. Joy felt like betrayal. If he couldn't be happy, how dare we, or I?

When I left for college in D.C., my world collapsed. No more rules. No mother. No structure. I was emotionally unmoored. I fell hard into partying, drugs, and depression. I stayed up all night, slept all day, and skipped classes until my GPA plummeted to 0.25. I felt anxious, lost, and not worth saving.

That darkness never completely disappeared. It got lighter at times, and I got better at hiding it. I got married and had two kids. I built a successful career—became a top salesperson, launched a sales training business, and made good money.

Yet the fog never fully lifted. I got divorced when my girls were young. I was deeply afraid of intimacy. Letting someone in felt dangerous. What if they left, too?

Still, I was lucky. I was loved. Remarkable women stood by me and supported me. I also had real friends and my family to support me. And I found joy in moments: traveling, listening to music, laughing, being with my girls, and more. But something at my core was still unresolved.

Until I went to India.

About twenty-five years ago, I visited an ashram with my second wife, Puja, who had lived there for years. One afternoon, I lay on a massage table sweating, the air thick with heat. A woman massaged me—deep, silent, rhythmic, present. And suddenly, I broke. I began to sob. Deep, guttural, unstoppable sobs. My whole body convulsed.

And through it all, one sentence repeated itself, "Dad, I have to let you go. I'm so sorry, but I have to."

In that moment, something broke open. I wasn't just crying; I was releasing something. I had carried his pain all these years, trying to earn love by sharing in his suffering. But now, I was letting it go. Not with anger. With grief. With compassion.

And then, something lifted. The shadow I had lived in began to fade. For the first time, I felt joy—not borrowed, not conditional. Just joy!

JONATHAN LONDON is a Queens, NYC-born sales leader; lifelong spiritual seeker; devoted father, grandfather, and sibling; and now the creator of a podcast that blends mindfulness and the art of selling.

Life's Not Punishing You, It's Growing You

I'm a strategic coach for entrepreneurs and executives who want to unlock their full potential. I never ask my clients to do the hard work I'm not committed to doing myself.

Posts like this one that I shared on LinkedIn are how I quietly measure my own growth and how I notice the full-circle moments that mark real transformation. And if it offers a gentle nudge to someone else on their path, all the better.

***

Had a full circle moment last week.
Still sitting with it.

It started with a memory
I hadn't thought about in years.

Ten years ago,
I was a mess.

Chaotic on the inside.
Clinging to outside validation.
No belief in myself.
Brittle.

Then I lost it all.
And felt even more lost.

I remember this one trip to New York.
I drank too much every night.
Told myself I was celebrating.
But really?
I was just coping.

New Year's Day.
Hungover.
Crawled to the hotel restaurant for caffeine.

The manager—
Guy about my age now—
Kept saying this over and over:

"New Year, New Me."
"I'm going to do things differently this year."

At first, I hated it.
My head was pounding.
I just wanted silence.

But by my second cup of coffee,
I started whispering it too.

"New Year, New Me."
"Do things differently."

I wish I could say
everything changed that day.

But transformation is rarely instant.

It's slow.
Intentional.
Sometimes painful.

Last week,
I went back to that same hotel.
That same restaurant.
That same bar stool.

The manager wasn't there.
But I was.

And the Stephen drinking coffee now?
Nothing like the Stephen from ten years ago.

New decade. New me.

Because I really did start doing things differently.

In small ways:

- I stopped needing all the answers.
- I got curious.
- I stopped reverting to fear.
- I welcomed the unknown.
- I stopped trying to be like everybody else.
- I became my own damn self.

There are really only two kinds of people:

Those who hit conflict
and refuse to change.

And those who hit conflict
and recognize it for what it really is:

An invitation to transform.

If life feels hard right now,
the universe isn't punishing you.

It's trying to grow you.

Because you have no idea
how magnificent you really are.

STEPHEN MOEGLING, founder of Band of Misfits®, is a strategic coach who helps entrepreneurs and leaders scale smarter, lead with bigger impact, and create more space for what matters.

Chapter 21
Finding Fullness

Pivotal moments are life moments, too. We often face regrets and encounter ongoing issues and challenges in our careers or with our families. But ultimately, we can find happiness and success and even be grateful for the journey we've been on.

The Hole in My Heart

The challenging aspect of being a businesswoman is that you must still find fulfillment in your personal life. Being a mother had always been part of the plan. But for the first two decades of my career, the dream eluded me. I was too late.

I tried. I went to the fertility clinic. I even married a man who should have remained my hiking buddy. But in December 2003, at the age of forty-two, I stood near a merry-go-round in a park when the nurse called.

"You're not pregnant," she said.

I'd prayed and hoped. But in that moment, I knew I was done. No more shots. No more pills. No more dreams of Sunday school lessons and lullabies.

I'd focus on work. That was my reality.

My mother had always told me not to mourn when plans didn't unfold as I'd hoped.

"We're not really in control," she'd say.

The hiker and I divorced. A year later, I met Lee. We married. Still, something was missing. I just felt … absent. Like I was going through the motions of a life that looked full but felt faint.

I told my doctor, "I don't know if I need to go on a cleanse, write a book, change careers, volunteer in India, or become a full-time yogi." She prescribed an antidepressant. I never picked it up, because before anything could change, everything did.

My phone rang. "She's dead," my husband said. "Tyler's mother was killed today."

His son, Tyler—my stepson—had lost his mom in a bicycle accident just hours earlier. And just like that, I became a full-time mother overnight.

We packed up our lives in Park City and moved to California, so Tyler wouldn't have to change schools or lose more than he already had.

I was terrified.

The next few months as a new mother would be the most agonizing, self-sacrificing, helpless period of my life. Everything I cooked had too much egg, not enough cheese, or lacked some mysterious ingredient. My husband and I stopped curling up at night with wine and our favorite shows.

Then, one pivotal moment shifted everything.

We'd started a ritual—campfires in the front yard under the trees, roasting marshmallows. That night, I congratulated Tyler on making it through his first whole week back at school since the accident.

"I'm proud of you," I said.

He looked down at his marshmallow and said, "I still miss my mommy."

"You'll miss her for a long time," I replied. "Sometimes it feels like a hole in your heart. Grown-ups have those too. But they can heal."

He looked at me. "Do you have a hole in your heart?"

"Yes," I said softly. "Because I never had children of my own."

He asked questions—about the shots, the pills, the "vitro." Then he went quiet.

Finally, he looked at me and said, "The hole in my heart would be a lot bigger if you weren't my stepmom."

I tried to hold back the tears. But something shifted inside me. All the pain, all the questions, all the years of aching—gone.

"Tyler," I said, "that's the nicest thing anyone's ever said to me. I think you just filled the hole in my heart."

Tyler is nearly twenty-one now. I adopted him a few years back. He's my son in every way that matters—and the greatest gift I never knew I was waiting for.

Not long ago, I found an old journal entry from that December day near the merry-go-round.

I asked my husband, "When was Tyler conceived?"

He paused, thinking. "Right before Christmas," he said. "December 2003."

My mother always told me we're not really in control. She was right. Because sometimes, the universe answers our prayers—just not in the way we expected.

SHARI LEVITIN is a sales futurist and bestselling author who helps teams grow by blending AI with human connection, guided by her belief: to sell more, you must be more.

The Gift of Rejection

There's a moment in everyone's life that changes the direction of the road they're on. For me, that moment came during a quiet conversation with the dean of a medical school—a conversation that at first felt like a door slamming shut but turned out to be something far more valuable.

I had done everything right, or so I thought. I had pushed hard through college, packed in summer classes, and graduated early with honors and a degree in English. Along the way, I checked every box required for medical school—premed courses, MCATs, and recommendation letters.

I wasn't at the very top of my class, but I was close. I thought I had earned my seat in the next incoming class at the university's medical school.

So, when the letter came saying I hadn't been accepted—but was placed on the alternate list—I was crushed. The kind of crushed that sits heavy in your chest and clouds your future. I couldn't understand why. My scores and grades matched up with many who had gotten in. I needed answers.

That's what led me to Dr. Al Sullivan, the dean of the medical school. He was known for telling it like it is, and I figured I had nothing to lose. When I sat across from him and asked, "Why wasn't I accepted?" he didn't hesitate.

He looked at me calmly and said, "You've been a student for sixteen years. You know how to do that well. But you haven't lived life yet. Go experience it, then come back."

I walked out of his office with no acceptance letter, but with something far more important: direction.

So, I stepped out into the world—not as a student, but as a person trying to figure out who I was. I worked in hospitals as a nurse's aide, caring for children with cancer. I saw heartbreak and resilience. I cleaned operating rooms and caught glimpses of surgeries in progress.

I got married. We saved up enough money to travel across Europe and came home to start a family. We had two daughters. I became a high school English teacher, trying to spark a love of literature in students who'd rather be anywhere else. I coached tennis and track. I even drove a school bus and spent a summer elbow-deep in a wastewater treatment plant.

At one point, we lived in a farmhouse where I chopped wood and learned how to dig silage out of a silo. The older couple who owned the land became like family to us—offering wisdom, warmth, and reminders of a slower, more meaningful life.

Six years passed.

Then one day, the memory of that conversation with Dr. Sullivan came back to me. That desire to become a doctor still lived deep inside. I made another appointment with him and asked if I still had a chance. He smiled and told me, "Now you've got the experience to be a great doctor. Retake the MCAT. Show us you're ready."

So, I studied on my own, retook the test, and scored just as well—if not better—than before. Not long after, a new letter came.

"We are pleased to offer you a place in the entering class of medical school."

This time, the door opened.

Looking back, I realize those years between rejection and acceptance were a gift. They didn't make me a smarter doctor, maybe. But they made me a better one. More importantly, they made me a better person.

So here's to disappointments—and to the people who are brave enough to tell us to go live life. Thank you, Dr. Sullivan. You changed everything.

KEITH BECKER is a retired ENT (Ear, Nose, and Throat) specialist who travels the world, studies birds in their natural habitats, writes books in his spare time, and still plays tennis.

Thank God I Didn't Get the Scholarship

There was a period of about three years in college when I was absolutely convinced that I was going to become a federal prosecutor. I dreamt of bringing down mob bosses and domestic terrorists with nothing but words.

By my junior year, I'd worked my way into a prestigious summer fellowship at a name-brand school in Cambridge, Massachusetts. It came with a rotation of political and public service internships.

This particular fellowship also put me in great position to win a Truman Scholarship—the US equivalent to the Rhodes Scholar program. Even better, it would provide a full ride to law school.

After that summer, I got amazing news: I was selected as a Truman finalist. The last hurdle was an interview. I'm great at interviews. This was a lock.

One little catch with the Truman Scholarship is that it's not exactly free. You get a full ride, but only if you commit to entering a public service job for five years. If you leave, you pay it all back. No problem.

I had convinced myself that government work was exactly what I wanted. Never mind the occasional doubts that crept in or the fact that I fell asleep next to my internship boss—an assistant attorney general—while at a telecom deposition. Surely real lawyering would be more exciting.

I prepared as well as I thought I needed to for the big interview; the format was basically seven high-achieving public servants (federal judges, former governors) assaulting the interviewee with questions like:

- What's your favorite US Supreme Court case?
- Oh, Marbury v. Madison? Make the case that it was actually the wrong decision.

Turns out, I was not prepared. I got shellacked. I knew before I left the interview I wasn't going to win.

Several of the people from my fellowship program did win Trumans, and I was left contemplating what to do with, you know, the rest of my life.

I won't say I was bereft or anything, but I was more disappointed by it than anything up until that point in my academic career.

Over the years, I've followed the careers of my friends who won the scholarship. They took extremely similar paths: grad school, federal job, climb the ladder.... retire? I'm not sure, because we're only in our forties.

With the benefit of some hindsight, I've grown so thankful I didn't win it. All the signs were there that I was not cut out for that kind of work.

Had I won, I would have served the minimum five-year sentence and probably another ten out of duty before I lost my mind (or fell asleep next to another boss).

And I would have missed out on the unpredictable, circuitous career that brought me from nonprofits to tech startups.

I won't say that I don't suffer from disappointments anymore, but the blows are softened knowing that sometimes you get exactly what you deserve.

JOSH LABAU is an artificial intelligence engineer and language lover who builds tools for storytellers.

The Day I Left for Good

I'm nineteen years old and about to jump out of the passenger door of a moving automobile so I can get my life back.

The driver is my abuser, who is also my husband. We've been married for less than a year, and I have a baby who, at that moment, is safely with my parents.

Many times, he's told me that if I leave him, he'll kill me. It seems to me that, at least for now, I will have control over how and when I go—if, in fact, I'd even be hurt jumping out that door.

Three, two, one.

I quickly open my door as he's driving toward an intersection, and BAM—I roll out cleanly and keep moving off the road toward the sidewalk.

Someone slows down and pulls over. "Are you OK? Need help?"

My husband Jessie, who also pulls over, yells. "Keep going, man. Everything's fine."

Again, the stranger asks, "Do you need me to call anyone?"

My husband shouts, "Keep going!"

The stranger drives away. I'm stuck. No one else is around.

Since this is the day I've decided is my last day of abuse, I dust myself off and tell Jessie to drive us back to my parents' house, where our son is visiting.

I say that I'll run in, get him, and we can head home.

This is one of the many white lies an abused woman gives her abuser to get out of a jam. I'd previously suffered bruises, cuts, choking, and broken bones. Today is the last day. My mind is made up.

We arrive at my parents' house, and I say, "I'll be right back."

Once inside, I know I'm done. I call the police and hear myself telling my parents that I'm not leaving for a while. They seem relieved, knowing a bit of the back story.

My infant son sleeps, oblivious to the situation. He will never remember the physical or mental abuse I've dealt with. He will break the cycle of abuse on his dad's side of the family.

This is a life-or-death decision I'm making. I made it.

Often, I told God that if I were to get away alive, I'd put all my power to good use to help others. It is a deal I don't take lightly.

Now I gather the pieces of my life—our lives—because I now have this little innocent child who did not ask to be involved in this. We move forward one step at a time.

My abusive husband will go home after a talk with the police. After leaving and returning twice more, it's over. Finally.

I am now embarking on the next chapter of my life as a single mom. I'm excited for what the future holds and for keeping the deal I made alive.

LORI RICHARDSON, founder of Score More Sales, is a sales strategist working with company leaders to bring in helpful AI processes to improve company revenue results.

Love Makes a Family: The Story of JJ

Families are shaped in many ways—by choice, by chance, and sometimes by quiet perseverance. Our family's journey has been defined by all three.

One of our sons and his wife chose not to have children. Their decision was thoughtful and deliberate, rooted in values they hold dear. Though it diverged from tradition, it was filled with purpose and integrity. They lead a full and meaningful life, and their choice has our total respect.

Our other son and his wife had a deep longing to become parents. They tried for years—through natural means, through IVF—facing disappointment after disappointment. The pain of infertility is quiet but consuming. Despite every effort, parenthood seemed just out of reach.

Yet they never gave up. They registered for adoption in multiple cities across the country, enduring months of waiting, hoping, and preparing their hearts. And then one day, five months into their search, a call came from a hospital in Houston.

"We have a baby for you."

The birth mother was young and already caring for another child. She knew she couldn't give this baby the life he deserved. With courage and love, she chose adoption.

My son and daughter-in-law traveled to Houston, hearts full and hands ready. There they met their son—tiny, fragile, and full of potential. They named him Johnny, or JJ for short.

From the moment he arrived, JJ changed everything.

He is now a whirlwind of energy and enthusiasm, with bottomless curiosity about the world. Whether he's exploring a bug in the backyard or asking questions far beyond his years, JJ craves attention, interaction, and understanding.

He wants adults to engage with him, to be part of his discoveries. He challenges us to keep up—and delights us with his cleverness, his laughter, and his boundless spirit.

This fall, JJ starts private school. It's a new chapter, full of promise. We watch with pride and anticipation as he begins his formal learning journey, knowing that his mind and heart are already so alive with questions.

Our family doesn't look like we once imagined it might. One son built a life without children. One son became a father through adoption.

And now, in the center of it all, is JJ—our bright, bouncing, curious grandson—reminding us that love makes a family, and that sometimes the most beautiful stories are the ones we never saw coming.

CARLOS QUINTERO, founder of Sales Effectiveness, Inc. and EKG Power, helps organizations drive superior customer experiences. He's an active family man and now enjoying the world of being a grandpa!

He Left Me for Eight Months

One of the most difficult things I've ever faced occurred in early 1955. We'd been living in Massachusetts, where my husband, Harold, was assigned to the Coast Guard District office. Then, he received orders to report to the USCG Cutter Kukui based in Hawaii.

We left right after New Year's Day. At that time, David was twenty-six months old, and Judy was only four months old. To get there, we first traveled across the US by car, stopping to see family and friends on the way.

Then we sailed from Fort Mason in San Francisco aboard the USNS Ainsworth. After five days, we arrived at Pearl Harbor. We were greeted with leis and warm welcomes. Then we were taken to transient quarters until we could find housing.

Fortunately, we found a two-bedroom townhouse in Moanalua Military Housing near Pearl Harbor. But our furniture shipment hadn't arrived yet, so we borrowed Navy furniture and moved in.

Harold's ship, the Kukui, was leaving in early February; he was going to be gone for almost eight months. But first he had to fly to the Philippines to get the site ready, people hired, etc. before the ship arrived.

He left just three days after our furniture arrived. Then, our car came three days after that. I didn't know how to drive!

This was one of the most difficult, terrifying moments of my life. The husband I adored was gone for eight months. I had two small children I had to keep safe. I made every bit of food and changed every diaper. I was living in a completely new place and had a vehicle that I didn't know how to drive.

A thoughtful Coast Guard warrant officer picked up our car from the docks and drove it to our home. An extremely kind Japanese woman came to our house to give me driving lessons while her husband babysat. In a short time, I was issued a driver's license from the Territory of Hawaii.

Moanaloa Military Housing, where we lived, was for junior officers and their families. Ages ranged from early twenties to late thirties. There were loads of children and MANY pregnant wives. A lot of the time, the husbands were gone on assignments in the Pacific.

Since many of us were alone a lot, we developed close, caring friendships. Almost daily, after doing our chores, we'd gather in someone's yard or apartment to have coffee. Four or five children would be playing nearby.

In those prehistoric days, children were not allowed in the commissary, so we'd take turns sitting with the children so that another friend could get her grocery shopping done.

There were a few difficult times when a neighbor's husband was killed in a plane crash or some other accident. That was when we would gather to support the wife through her grief and subsequent move.

As I look back on that terrifying time when Harold left for eight months, I realize it was a time when I matured. In short, I became a strong, independent woman.

I learned to drive! I learned and appreciated the closeness and support of military wives. I took care of all our paperwork and paid the bills on time! Most importantly, I took care of two beautiful children, kept them happy, and developed a loving bond with them.

It was a wonderful day when we were on the dock, welcoming Harold home. I recognize, however, that during that separation, my fears had turned into a certainty that I could cope with the difficulties I would encounter throughout the rest of my life.

JANELLEN DECKER BROCK, born in 1930, is still intensely interested in others, seeking to learn from them and help them. She's active in church, community groups, aquacize, and more. She remains fiercely independent.

PART 5
Springing Forward

Chapter 22
Taking Action

Embracing our pivotal moments is both challenging and life-changing. These triggering events offer us an opportunity to gain a deeper insight into ourselves and what really matters to us. They also help us envision different possibilities for our future.

As you have seen from the stories shared in the previous section, life is full of pivotal moments. They come in all sorts of shapes and sizes.

Sometimes you need to restart yourself after hitting the wall. Or you get kicked out of your comfort zone and are flailing—and don't know what you'll do next.

Other times, you have an idea that you really want to implement—but are overwhelmed with "how." You might hear something that alters your perspective of yourself, your situation, or your future. You start thinking beyond the present and enter the "what's really possible" zone.

But what we often don't realize is that frequently, there are numerous hidden opportunities within these pivotal moments.

As you work through the challenges you face, you build strengths you didn't realize you had. Sometimes, you even surprise yourself. You form new friendships, discover new opportunities, and ultimately recognize that you're stronger than you thought. It's all good!

But taking a step into the unknown requires more than courage. That's why I created the Pivotal Moment Workbook for you. I've also created some additional resources for you, including videos, interviews, and articles.

You can access them all by scanning the QR code below or going to:

www.WhatsReallyPossible.com/pm-resources

I guarantee you'll get more fresh ideas and be inspired to take action. So hop to it!

Acknowledgements

I'd like to express my sincere gratitude to my family and circle of friends for their unwavering support and encouragement throughout the various pivotal moments in my life. You've helped me through the inevitable, but still unexpected, speed bumps in the road. It's been quite a journey!

Also, a big thank you to all the individuals who allowed me to share their stories in this book. As you'll see, their pivotal moments are deeply personal. Sometimes they're shattering. Other times, they're eye-opening.

Yet each person grasped onto the challenge they faced and used it as a turning point in their life. The result? A better future. So thank you, thank you, thank you to:

Angela Botiba, Risa August, Melinda Emerson, Todd Johnson, Joanne Black, Ardath Albee, Dao Jensen, Orrin Broberg, Lori Chester, Dawn Epstein, Michael Nelson, Colleen Stanley, Dan Tyre, Joe Yun, Lori Harris, Yuliia Yurchuk, Luke Goetting, Dave Brock, Tom Morris, Colleen Kranz, Robert Middleton, Jonathan London, Stephen Moegling, Shari Levitin, Keith Becker, Josh LaBau, Lori Richardson, Carlos Quintero, and Janellen Brock.

Your personal stories are powerful and inspiring to all of us.

About the Author

Jill Konrath inspires positive change in an evolving world. Recently, she launched her "What's Really Possible" initiative to help people leverage today's pivotal moments as springboards to a better future.

Over 1/3 million people follow her on LinkedIn and read her newsletter. She's a conduit of fresh strategies, practical ideas, and uncommonly good sense mixed with humor and humility.

Jill has written four best-selling books and spoken at conferences worldwide. She's been hailed as the #1 LinkedIn sales thought leader multiple times, featured in a sales documentary, and quoted in *Forbes*, *Fortune*, *Inc.*, *Entrepreneur*, *New York Times*, and *Wall Street Journal*.

www.ingramcontent.com/pod-product-compliance
Lightning Source LLC
Chambersburg PA
CBHW032226080426
42735CB00008B/729